W9-CLB-387

CHESTER CHOWDER

CHESTER CHOWDER
A Potpourri of Nova Scotia Recipes

Compiled and Edited By
JANET ONDAATJE

Pagurian Press Limited
TORONTO

Copyright ©1982 The Pagurian Corporation Limited
13 Hazelton Avenue, Toronto, Canada

Copyright under the Berne Convention. All rights reserved. No part of this book may be reproduced in any form without the permission of the publishers.

Illustrations by Sarah Ondaatje

ISBN 0-88932-121-3 (casebound edition)
ISBN 0-88932-122-1 (paperback edition)

Printed and Produced in Canada by:
Centax Books, A Division of PrintWest Communications Ltd.
1150 Eighth Avenue, Regina, Saskatchewan,
Canada S4R 1C9
(306) 525-2304   FAX (306) 757-2439

For the young people of Bonny Lea Farm, a unique residential and training facility designed for the rehabilitation of the multiple handicapped, to whom all profits of this book will be donated.

Daydream

My heart is not on Highland
Nor that tanned Bermuda island
And remembering Ceylon is hard for me.
And my heart is not on Bay Street
Where the moguls run 'round bare feet
When you've been there once that's all there is to see.

And my love is not in England
I don't like a Queen and King land
Pomp and circumstance are far too much for me.
And Europe's just too distant
One can't get there in an instant
The price for freedom's much too high a fee.

Give me taste of salt and windswept
Lifting fog and lilting sunset
Sailing down Back Harbour, out but back for tea.
Berry picking on the hillside
Boats moored carefree, low and high tide
And the sound of gulls, that's where I want to be.

I can feel the mist rise slowly
And the plaintive loon call lowly
Oh! I pray one day I can afford the fee.
Just to buy a one-way ticket
Far from crowded city thicket
Down to Chester, Nova Scotia, by the sea.

Christopher Ondaatje

Contents

Bonny Lea Farm

History of Bonny Lea Farm

Throughout the late sixties and early seventies it was becoming evident that the needs of and opportunities for Lunenburg County children with special needs were not being provided. A group of friends and concerned citizens gathered one evening, and thus began a series of planning meetings designed to consider the problem and to implement services to these young people. So it was that the South Shore Community Service Association came to be born. In the autumn of 1972, classes for children, who were being by-passed by educational opportunity, began in the Masonic Hall in Chester which served as a classroom for seven students, their teacher, and her aide, a certified nursing assistant.

Physically speaking Bonny Lea Farm is a complex of buildings situated on a beautiful meadow ("Bonny Lea" in the language of the Scots) on the Windsor Road a few blocks from Exit 8 off of Highway # 103. About five miles to the southeast is the town of Chester, Nova Scotia. Rolling hills and the sparkling blue of Mahone Bay, interspersed with tree-clad islands, are within the limits of its vistas.

Bonny Lea Farm began operations in its current location in 1973, under the auspices of the South Shore Community Service Association. It was designed primarily to serve multi-handicapped, special-needs young people of school age. Bonny Lea fulfilled the need for the special education opportunities that had not yet been mandated by the Province as the specific responsibility of the Department of Education, and so it continued for 11 years. In 1984 all school-age children were integrated into the "mainstream" of the Department's facilities. In consequence, Bonny Lea Farm underwent a transition period to determine the population that most needed to be served and how those services might best be delivered.

Currently Bonny Lea serves adults with special needs who are physically, emotionally, behaviourally or mentally challenged by virtue of birth or accident. Our mission is to promote personal growth and dignity and through training to provide opportunities for meaningful work, personal dignity, and productive independent living. The programs at Bonny Lea fall under four major categories: The Vocational Program, Support Services, Vocational Evaluation and the Center for Independent Living. These activities sponsored by the association have as their common and continuing goal the encouragement and stimulation of maximum intellectual, physical, emotional, social and spiritual development of each participant. Wherever appropriate our aim is the return of a participant to the environmental surroundings most suitable for the continuance of his or her further growth and development.

A large portion of the funds necessary to operate our programs depends upon the goodwill of friends and foundations. We welcome all who would like to visit with us and have an opportunity to see for themselves what happens in our day-to-day living. At Bonny Lea Farm love and caring abound; every handicap is met as a challenge and every individual is provided with opportunities for self-enrichment, personal dignity and productive living.

Foreword

I am proud to have been asked to introduce what I consider to be not only a truly remarkable book but a remarkable achievement. Janet Ondaatje has worked both enthusiastically and creatively to make this fund raising idea for Bonny Lea Farm a reality. In doing so she has produced a cookbook that belongs in every home proud of its Maritime traditions.

Canada is an enormous country with a varied mixture of people. Traditionally there is the French and English influence, but there have developed other truly Canadian influences stemming from the many ethnic groups who have settled here. *Chester Chowder* is a book that makes fascinating reading as it includes the recipes and table traditions of not only the French and English — but the Germans, Scots, American, Irish, Dutch, and other peoples who have made their homes in the area. There is a regional style of cooking in Chester — Hodgepodge, Salt Cod Soup, Spare Ribs with Apples and Sauerkraut, Cabbage Chowder, Dandelion Greens, Dutchman's Special, Pork and Codfish Fry, South Shore Fish Bake, Tancook Raw Potato Hash, Anadama Bread, Scotch Woodcock, Sausage Pie, and Blueberry Buckle, to name but a few. You will be amazed, as you leaf through this book, at how the recipes embody the character of the people and the hardy way of life in this historical maritime village.

Many thanks are due to Janet and Pagurian Press for producing this ambitious community project. The recipes, and the character that the recipes reveal, provide an interesting and extremely useful culinary document.

★*Bertie Baker,*
Bonny Lea Farm,
Chester, Nova Scotia

Introduction

As one travels south from Halifax, or east from Lunenburg, one will discover the tiny, picturesque seaside village of Chester (now called the Municipality of the District of Chester). This small fishing and lumbering town was once described as an artist's haven and all it takes is one quick glance over the rolling hills to the ocean to realize that this is unquestionably so. The expanse, complex maze of shoals, rocks and islands, provides an unspoiled paradise for those who visit and for those who live here year round.

It was the placid deep channels, beaches and quiet simplicity that attracted many New Englanders just ten years after the founding of Halifax in 1749. At the head of Mahone Bay and east of Martin's River, Timothy Haughton and William Keynes received one of the first strips of land (about 100,000 acres). Many of the settlers, having abandoned their homes in Massachusetts, Vermont, Maine and New Hampshire, brought spinning wheels, pots, pans, furniture, — everything, preparing for the new life that awaited them in Acadia. This sparsely settled area was called the township of Shoreham; but was shortly afterwards changed to Chester in honour of the Earl of Chester who was one of the Lords of Trade and Plantation. The beautiful town of Chester was eventually to become one of the loveliest summer resorts and famous yachting centres in North America.

As big cities were sprouting up all over the continent, Chester remained virtually undeveloped and, to this day, still retains much of the culture, customs and charm that existed almost two and a half centuries ago. Many of the families of the original settlers and their homes still exist, as do countless recipes that have been handed down from generation to generation. This book contains many of these traditional dishes, and also many that have been brought to Chester over the years from different corners of the world, and many that have been adapted to the unique style of living that exists in this casual but proud Nova Scotia hamlet.

I would like to thank all those who helped me with this book, contributed recipes, and who shared their family histories. Thank you also for making me feel part of this pretty and historic little town.

Janet Ondaatje

★ *Janet Ondaatje*

Hors d'oeuvre

COLD ASPARAGUS IN MUSTARD SAUCE

A wonderful beginning to a festive spring dinner.

1½ to 2 pounds fresh asparagus, cleaned and and tied into bundles
1 egg, hard-boiled
1 raw egg yolk
1½ teaspoons Dijon mustard
½ cup olive oil
1½ tablespoons white wine vinegar

1 to 2 tablespoons well-drained capers
salt and white pepper
6 to 8 cooked medium shrimp, peeled and deveined (optional garnish)
vinaigrette dressing (optional)
1 tablespoon parsley, minced

Bring about 4 cups salted water to boil in 6-quart pan. Add asparagus and cook uncovered 10 to 12 minutes, or just until tender. Run immediately under cold water to stop further cooking and to retain color. Set aside to cool but do not refrigerate.

Separate hard-boiled egg, reserving yolk; finely mince white. Blend hard-boiled yolk, raw yolk and mustard in blender or food processor until smooth. Slowly add oil, beating until thick and creamy. Blend in vinegar. Transfer to a small bowl. Add capers. Season with salt and white pepper.

Place asparagus on serving dish. Spoon sauce over, leaving tips exposed. If using shrimp garnish, dress with vinaigrette and place over mustard sauce. Sprinkle with egg white and parsley. Serve at room temperature. Serves 4-6.

★*Mrs. John Fraser*

SPINACH SQUARES

A great favourite at summer cocktail parties.

1/4	cup butter or margarine	2	teaspoons salt
3	eggs	2	packages chopped spinach, thawed and well drained
1	cup flour		
1	cup milk	1	pound cheddar cheese, cut into small squares

Preheat oven to 350°F. Melt butter in 9 x 13-inch glass dish. Beat eggs and stir in remaining ingredients. Pour into dish and mix with butter. Bake 30-40 minutes. Cut in squares for appetizers. Serve hot or cold.

★*Sally Farrell*

PRINCE SCHWARZENBERG'S ARABIAN SAUCE

Good with cocktails and conversation.

1/2	pound mixed nuts	1	teaspoon dry mustard
1/2	cup onions, chopped		cream or milk
1	clove garlic, minced		red pepper
1	tablespoon sesame or olive oil		salt, to taste

Grind nuts with onion and garlic. Add oil, vinegar and mustard and blend together. Add cream or milk if sauce is too thick. Season with salt and pepper. Refrigerate. Serve with crackers. Yield: approximately 2 cups.

★*Martha Woolley*

SHRIMP SEA ISLAND

A little messy to eat, but a very good-tasting appetizer.

2	pounds large raw shrimp	2	tablespoons capers
	salt	1	lemon, finely sliced
$^1/_2$	cup vinegar	2	onions, sliced
$^1/_2$	teaspoon whole peppercorns	$^1/_4$ to $^1/_3$ cup olive oil	

Peel shrimp and remove back membrane. Try to leave the tail shells on, as they look attractive and shrimps can be picked up by them.

Put shrimps in a double boiler with salt only, no water. Cook until done, about half an hour. Boil the vinegar. When cold, add sugar, salt to taste, peppercorns, capers, lemon and onion slices. Add shrimps and some good olive oil. Put this in the bowl you intend to serve it in and refrigerate for 24 hours. Tooth picks may be used to spear shrimps.

★*Marian Straus*

PECAN CHEESE PARTY BALL

The pecans give a satisfying richness and a slight nutty flavour to this dish.

3 ounces Roquefort cheese	**2 tablespoons chopped onion**
$1/_2$ (8 ounces) container Imperial cheddar spread	**$1/_4$ cup coarsely chopped parsley**
250-gram package (8 ounces) cream cheese	**$1/_2$ teaspoon Worcestershire sauce**
2-ounce package ($1/_2$ cup) pecan halves	

Place cheeses in blender or food processor. Add rest of ingredients and whirl, using an on-and-off motion, until the nuts are finely chopped and the cheeses well mixed. Press in container and refrigerate. May be frozen. Serve at room temperature with crackers or bread slices.

★*Marion Mulrooney*

MELTED CHEESE HORS D'OEUVRE

Always popular at cocktail parties.

bread, sandwich size	**chutney**
grated mozzarella or	**spring onions, finely**
cheddar cheese	**chopped**
mayonnaise	**bacon bits**
Worcestershire sauce	

Cut crusts from bread and then cut each slice into four squares. Place bread on cookie sheet. Mix all ingredients in a bowl. Use your own discretion as to amounts, according to how many you make. Don't add too much mayonnaise, or, when cheese melts, it will be greasy rather than gooey. Heat in oven until melted and golden brown. This takes approximately 12 to 15 minutes.

★*Mary T. Grant*

HOMEMADE BOURSIN

Mix this up in the morning, and by cocktail time it'll be ready. Serve with crackers.

8 ounces cream cheese	**$1/_4$ teaspoon dill**
$1/_4$ pound sweet butter	**$1/_4$ teaspoon marjoram**
$1/_4$ teaspoon basil	**black pepper, freshly**
$1/_4$ teaspoon thyme	**ground**
	garlic salt, to taste

Mix well, put into crock to serve.

★*Lu Ann Polk*

VERMOUTH CHEESE CROCK

Great to make ahead, either for at home or on a cruise!

1	pound old cheddar cheese	2	cloves garlic
3	ounces cream cheese	1	teaspoon dry mustard
4	ounces blue cheese	4	drops Tabasco
$^1/_4$	pound butter	$^1/_2$	cup sweet Vermouth

Place all ingredients in blender and process until well mixed. Place in a container and keep refrigerated until needed. Serve with your favourite crackers.

★*Marion Mulrooney*

CHEESE FILLING

The important thing to remember about this recipe is to make sure the custard is thick before adding the cheese.

4	eggs, well beaten	$^1/_4$	cup vinegar
$^3/_4$	cup sugar	1	pound processed cheese
4	teaspoons dry mustard	1	tin pimento
$^1/_3$	cup butter	1	green pepper
	pinch of salt		

Combine eggs, sugar, mustard, butter and salt, and cook in a double boiler until it becomes a thick custard. Then, slowly, add vinegar and cook until thickened again. Add cheese, cut into small pieces, and stir until it melts and becomes smooth. Chop pimento and green pepper and add to cheese mixture. Pour into a decorative crock and surround with crackers. Serve as an appetizer. This spread can also be used for sandwiches and can be stored in the refrigerator. It keeps very well.

★*Joan Rounsfell*

OHIO CHEESE BALL

A combination of flavours that goes well with a pre-dinner drink.

$1/_2$	pound Cheddar cheese	1	cup chopped parsley
$1/_4$	pound blue cheese	1	medium onion, grated fine
12	ounces cream cheese		dash Worcestershire sauce
1	cup chopped pecans		

Mix the Cheddar cheese, blue cheese and the cream cheese together. Add $1/_2$ cup pecans and $1/_2$ cup parsley and onion to cheese mix. Add Worcestershire sauce. Mix well. Form into 1 large or 2 small balls. Roll in remaining nut and parsley mix. Chill or freeze if desired.

★*Alberta Pew*

CRABMEAT MOULD

This crabmeat mould is a hit at all my summer gatherings.

1	can tomato soup	1	cup onion, finely chopped
1	envelope gelatin	2	cans crabmeat, mashed
1	cup mayonnaise		
1	cup celery, finely chopped		

Heat tomato soup slowly in double boiler, add gelatin, stirring until well dissolved. Add cream cheese, then mayonnaise to heated mixture. Stir until well dissolved and creamy, then add last three ingredients, stirring well. Fold in mould and chill. Unmould and serve with crackers.

★*Deborah Grant*

SHRIMP MOULD

As an appetizer, with drinks, this serves a crowd.

1 can shrimp soup	$1^1/_2$ tablespoons green onion, chopped
1 envelope gelatin, softened in $^1/_2$ cup cold water	$^3/_4$ cup celery, chopped fine
2 8-ounce packages cream cheese	2 6-ounce cans small deveined shrimp
1 cup mayonnaise	salt, pepper, to taste

Heat soup to boiling point. Add gelatin which has been softened in water. Mix. Add softened cream cheese and blend well. Cool slightly, add other ingredients and mix. Spoon into mould. Refrigerate for several hours. Unmould and serve with crackers. Can be frozen.

★*Kathleen Rowan-Legg*

LOBSTER OR CRABMEAT DIP

I cook this in a double boiler and keep it hot at low temperature until it is used.

1 tablespoon melted butter	1 egg yolk
1 tablespoon flour	$^1/_2$ to 1 cup light cream
1 teaspoon pepper	2 tins crabmeat or lobster
	2 tablespoons sherry

Combine butter, flour, pepper, egg yolk and cream and heat and stir until thick. Add crabmeat or lobster and sherry. Serve on hot toasts as an appetizer.

★*Deborah Grant*

SHRIMP SALAD MOULD

A very pretty hors d'oeuvre — a dish for relaxed entertaining.

1	can tomato soup	1	cup chopped celery (fine)
2	packages Knox gelatin	$^1/_4$	cup chopped green onions (scallions)
8	ounces cream cheese	$^1/_4$	teaspoon garlic salt
$1^1/_2$	cups mayonnaise	2	cans shrimp (mash with fork)

Beat cream cheese and mayonnaise until smooth. Dissolve gelatin in $^1/_4$ cup water — add to soup. Heat soup to lukewarm. Mix with cream cheese and mayonnaise. Add celery, onions, garlic and shrimp. Pour into mould. Refrigerate about 2 hours. Serve with crackers.

★*Dee Dee Blain*

NANCY'S SMOKED SALMON

A most unusual appetizer, with a very delicate, smoky flavour.

1 pound smoked salmon	**$^1/_2$ teaspoon salt**
12 scallions	**4 tomatoes, peeled and**
$^1/_4$ cup ice water (scant)	**chopped**

Soak salmon in cold water for an hour. Drain. Remove scales, skin and bones, and shred salmon finely. Chop scallions. Combine scallions, tomatoes, salt and salmon and blend slightly in processor or blender. Salmon, scallions and tomatoes should be separate. This is *not* a smooth spread. Serve with crackers.

★*Deborah Grant*

If you can keep your head when all about you
Are losing theirs and drinking all your rum
Don't worry 'cos tomorrow they'll feel awful
And you'll be laughing in the morning sun.

OREGON SALMON BALL

Serve chilled on crackers with a before-dinner drink.

2 cups salmon, fresh
   or tinned
1 8-ounce package
   softened cream cheese
1 tablespoon lemon juice
2 teaspoons grated onion

1 teaspoon horseradish
$1/_4$ teaspoon salt
$1/_4$ teaspoon liquid smoke
$1/_2$ cup chopped pecans
3 tablespoons snipped parsley

Remove skin and bones from salmon. Drain and flake. Mix pecans and parsley together. Mix salmon, cream cheese, lemon juice, grated onion, horseradish, salt and liquid smoke, and chill for several hours. Shape into ball (or balls) and roll in nut and parsley mix. Chill and serve with crackers. It may be frozen.

★*Alberta Pew*

CLAM DIP

Serve with potato chips or crackers. Decorate with parsley or dill.

1 tin clams
3 tablespoons clam liquid
   (approximately)
1 4-ounce package cream
   cheese

dash of onion salt, salt,
pepper, paprika
1 tablespoon lemon juice

Drain clams and chop into small pieces. Save the liquid. Cream cheese until fluffy. Add clams, lemon juice and other seasonings. Pour in clam liquid until dip is the right consistency for easy dipping.

★*Mrs. Dale Barkhouse*

CHICKEN LIVER PÂTÉ

This pâté tastes better when refrigerated for several days before serving.

1/2 cup chopped chives
1 pound chicken livers
6 tablespoons butter
1 tablespoon curry
   (or to taste)
   salt and pepper
   thyme

basil
marjoram
allspice
1/2 cup dry vermouth
1/4 cup sour cream

Cut up livers and sauté in butter. Don't overcook them; then mash or blend. Add seasonings and blend to desired consistency. Taste, and adjust seasoning. Blend in sour cream. Pour into crock.

★*Gail Fraser*

CURRY PUFFS

Delicious when served warm from the oven. The perfect appetizer.

2 garlic cloves, mashed
1 piece crystallized ginger, cut fine
1 1/2 teaspoons minced onion
1 1/2 to 2 tablespoons curry powder
2 tablespoons butter

1/2 pound ground beef
1 tablespoon fresh lime juice
1/2 teaspoon salt
2 packages pie pastry mix

Sauté garlic, ginger, onion and curry powder in butter for 5 minutes. Add meat and stir until meat loses red colour. Add lime juice and salt. Mix well. Cool. Roll pastry and cut into 2-inch rounds. Place $1/_2$ teaspoon meat mixture (heaping) on one round. Fold over around meat and use a fork to press edges together. Bake on an ungreased cookie sheet in a preheated 450°F. oven for about 15 minutes until nicely browned. Makes about 3 dozen.

★*Eleanor Seyffert*

When seated at the evening dinner table
'Midst shiny silver in the candle light
Remember when you start your conversation
First address the lady on your right.

ZUCCHINI APPETIZERS

An unusual, delicious appetizer — wonderful on cold, wet evenings.

4 small, unpared zucchini	$1/_2$ teaspoon seasoned salt
1 cup Bisquick	$1/_2$ teaspoon dried marjoram or
$1/_2$ cup finely chopped onion	oregano leaves
$1/_2$ cup grated Parmesan cheese	1 clove garlic (optional)
	dash pepper
2 tablespoons parsley, chopped	$1/_2$ cup vegetable oil
	4 eggs, slightly beaten
$1/_2$ teaspoon salt	

Preheat oven to 350°F. Split zucchini lengthwise and slice thinly (3-4 cups). Mix all ingredients. Spread in greased 13 x 9 x 2 inch pan. Bake until golden brown, about 35 minutes. Cut into squares. Serve hot.

★*Sally Farrell*

ITALIAN ANTIPASTO

This recipe was given to me by an Italian lady married to an Englishman, when we were living in the Dominican Republic. It is very good served on crackers as an appetizer.

2 or 3	small eggplants or	2	large tomatoes, cut small
1	large		small whole olives
	salt and pepper		capers
2	onions, chopped	1	cup vinegar
	olive or peanut oil		

Cut eggplants into small pieces, cover with salt and let stand for 2 hours. Drain. Put in frying pan with onion, cover with oil and cook until onions are tender. Drain off excess oil. Add tomatoes, capers, olives, vinegar, salt and pepper (quite a bit) and simmer for 10 minutes; pour into jars and cool.

★*Eleanor Seyffert*

CHILI CHIP DIP

A boon for the busy cook, this chili dip can be prepared in seconds.

1	package (4 ounces) cream cheese	$1^1/_2$	tablespoons prepared horseradish
$^1/_4$	cup mayonnaise	1	tablespoon pickle relish
$^1/_4$	cup chili sauce		

Soften cream cheese. Add mayonnaise, chili sauce, horseradish and relish. Mix well. Keep refrigerated until ready to serve with your favourite potato chips. Freezes well.

★*Marion Mulrooney*

MUSHROOM PLEASERS

I find I can make the shells two days before and store them in a tin. The mushroom sauce can also be made ahead of time, earlier in the day. Store in the refrigerator and reheat at the last moment. These are always a great hit at our summer parties.

1 package refrigerated biscuits (Butterflake)	$1^1/_2$ cups milk (or more)
$^1/_2$ pound fresh mushrooms, finely chopped	$^1/_4$ cup dry white wine or vermouth
2 tablespoons flour	salt and pepper, to taste
2 tablespoons butter	

Grease small (miniature) muffin tins; separate the biscuits and press into the tins to make a shell. Bake in 400°F. until golden. It will take approximately 10 minutes. Keep watching as they are thin and cook quickly.

Then, melt butter, add flour to make a roux and gently add milk and white wine to make a medium-thick sauce. Sauté finely chopped mushrooms in 1 teaspoon butter. Add salt and pepper and a squeeze of lemon juice and add to the sauce. Transfer to a double boiler to keep warm. Fill the muffin cups with the mixture and serve before dinner or for cocktails. This recipe can be made in advance and reheated. It makes 2 dozen.

★*Joan Rounsfell*

SOUR CREAM VEGETABLE DIP

Great for the dieter!

1 cup sour cream, the thicker the better	2 teaspoons chopped parsley
1/4 cup mayonnaise	2 teaspoons chopped chives
2 tablespoons finely chopped onion	2 eggs, hard boiled
1 clove garlic, finely minced	

Mix together everything except eggs, and store to meld flavours. Finely chop the whites of the eggs and add to the sour cream mixture. Just before serving, sieve the yolks and sprinkle on top for a garnish. Place in centre of large plate and surround with a selection of fresh vegetables, cut into bite-sized pieces. I use celery, green beans, carrots, cherry tomatoes, zucchini, broccoli, fresh mushrooms, and cucumbers.

★*Joan Rounsfell*

ARTICHOKE DIP

Your guests will ask for the recipe!

1 can artichoke hearts (not the marinated variety)	3/4 cup Parmesan cheese, grated garlic powder
3/4 cup mayonnaise	

Mash artichokes with fork, stir in mayonnaise and Parmesan cheese and a pinch of garlic powder. Bake at 350°F. for 20 minutes. Sprinkle with paprika and parsley.

★*Peggy McAlpine*

Soups

CITADEL HILL FISH CHOWDER

This recipe was given to me by Mort Pelham, a past Commodore and Secretary Treasurer of the Nova Scotia Schooner Association, who served it to 50 hungry schooner sailors on the wharf at Nor' West Cove in St. Margaret's Bay. He prepared the chowder at home, then re-heated it in a ten-gallon milk can set in a fish tub of boiling water over a fire on the beach. Not only is he a great sea-man but a master at improvising and cooking too!

	25 Servings	50 Servings	100 Servings
Haddock fillets	4 pounds	8 pounds	16 pounds
Water	1 quart	2 quarts	1 gallon
Bay Leaf	1 small	1 large	2
Potatoes, raw, diced	3 cups	6 cups	$2^1/_2$ quarts
Butter	$^1/_2$ pound	1 pound	2 pounds
Celery, diced	1 cup	2 cups	4 cups
Onion, thinly sliced	1 pint	1 quart	2 quarts
Salt	2 tablespoons	3-4 tablespoons	$^1/_4$-$^1/_3$ cup
Pepper	1 teaspoon	$1^1/_2$ teaspoons	1 tablespoon
Flour	$^1/_2$ cup	1 cup	2 cups
Milk	1 quart	2 quarts	1 gallon
Table cream	3 pints	1 quart	2 quarts
Parsley, chopped	$^1/_4$ cup	$^1/_2$ cup	1 cup

In a large pot combine haddock fillets, water and bay leaf. Simmer, uncovered, until fish flakes easily with a fork (approximately 10 minutes). Reserve stock.

Remove fish, set aside, add diced potatoes to fish stock and cook until tender. In a large saucepan, melt butter, add celery, onion and seasonings; sauté until tender, approximately 10 minutes. Stir in flour and cook for 4 to 5 minutes more.

Meanwhile, slowly heat milk until warm; remove from heat. Stir in cream and heat until warm but do not boil.

Add potato with fish stock to vegetable mixture. Stir gently. Add cooked fish.

Add milk and cream to fish and potato mixture. Heat until piping hot but do not boil. Remove bay leaf and garnish with parsley.

★*Willa Creighton*

THE LEADING WIND OPENING NIGHT CHOWDER

Originally served at an opening night party for Chester's Leading Wind puppet theatre, this chowder was a great hit, and I have been making it ever since.

1	tin frozen lobster	1	tin Campbell's Potato Soup (10 ounce can)
4	onions		
6	ounces unsalted butter	2	cans blend cream
			chives
			salt
			pepper

Sauté onions in 2 ounces butter until soft but not brown. Add potato soup, fill up can twice with blend and add, stirring gently all the time. Add the lobster (cut up) and the butter. Simmer very slowly for 15 minutes and serve with chopped chives on top. Serves 4.

★*Helen Dennis*

FISH CHOWDER

Quick, easy, delicious.

$^1/_2$ **pound chowder haddock
or haddock fillets**
1 large onion
3 tablespoons celery
$^1/_4$ **pound butter**

1 tin evaporated milk
1 tin potato soup
**1 pint blended (half and half)
cream**

Cook onion and celery in butter until soft but not brown. Simmer haddock in small amount of water until it can be broken into small pieces.

Combine all ingredients and simmer for 20 minutes. Add spices to taste — sweet basil, tarragon, marjoram, summer savory, etc. Serves 6.

★*Kathleen Rowan-Legg*

DIANA'S FISH CHOWDER

The shrimp and seafood seasoning make this an exceptionally good chowder.

5 cups water	1 teaspoon salt
4 medium potatoes, diced	1 teaspoon pepper
1 medium onion, diced	1$^1/_2$ teaspoons seafood
2 stalks celery, diced	seasoning (or to taste)
2 medium carrots, diced small	$^1/_8$ cup butter
	1 tablespoon parsley
1$^1/_2$ pounds haddock fillets, cut into pieces	1 cup canned evaporated milk
	scallops or lobster (optional)
4 ounces small frozen shrimp	

Heat water, add vegetables and cook until tender. Add haddock, shrimp, salt, pepper and seafood seasoning. Cook until fish is tender. Turn down heat, and just before serving add butter, parsley and milk. Heat but do not boil. Serves 10.

★*Diana Hilchie*

POACHED FISH CHOWDER

Easy to make, nutritious and good.

bacon (diced) or butter	fresh or frozen fish fillets
diced onion	salt and pepper
diced potatoes	milk
diced carrots	butter, size of walnut

Fry bacon or melt butter. Add onion pieces and cook slightly. Do not brown. Cover with water and cook. When nearly cooked, add fish, which has been cut into 2-inch strips. Place the fish on top of chowder. Cover pot and cook until fish flakes easily. Add milk and butter. Keep hot until ready to serve.

★*Leta Udall*

SCALLOP SOUP

Serve warm, not hot. The delicate flavour comes through this way.

1	quart water	¼	teaspoon dry mustard
¾	cup dry white wine	1½	teaspoons salt
1	shallot or 1 tablespoon scallion, thinly sliced	½	teaspoon pepper
		½	pound scallops
⅛	teaspoon saffron	¾	cup light cream
⅛	teaspoon curry	2	teaspoons chopped chives

In a non-aluminum 2-quart pot put the water, shallot, saffron, curry, mustard, salt, and pepper. Bring to a boil, cover and simmer 15 minutes. Add scallops, cover and simmer 5 minutes more.

Purée contents in a blender, half at a time. The scallops do not purée completely, but remain in tiny pieces. Return soup to the pot and add cream; stir thoroughly. Reheat, but do not boil.

When ladling soup from the pot make sure you stir up the bottom to include pieces of scallops which will have collected there. Pour into individual soup cups, and sprinkle with chives or paprika. Serve quite warm, but not hot. Serves 6.

★ *Sally Farrell*

MOTHER'S FISH CHOWDER

Crushed crackers added just before serving will make a thicker chowder — also, mussels, lobster, or scallops can be substituted for the clams.

1	pound haddock	1	teaspoon salt
1 to 2	cans clams	½	teaspoon pepper
6	medium potatoes	2	teaspoons sugar
4	medium onions	1	tin evaporated milk
⅛	pound butter		

Boil cut-up potatoes, onions and fish in small amount of water until tender. Add butter, salt and pepper. When butter melts, add clams and milk. Simmer for approximately 5 to 10 minutes until chowder is very hot, but not boiling. Just before serving add sugar. Serves 4 generously.

★ *Elizabeth Pellow*

MRS. P'S FISH CHOWDER

Scallops make this chowder particularly flavourful and rich-tasting.

2	pounds fresh fillets of haddock		An "egg" of butter, salt, ground pepper to taste
2	pounds scallops	1	quart whole milk
3	large or 5 small potatoes	1	tin undiluted Carnation milk
2	onions		

Cube potatoes and onions. Put on to boil in cold salted water to cover. When nearly tender, add fish and simmer until fish is cooked. Heat quart of milk and pour into mixture. Add butter. Put aside to cool slightly. Add Carnation. Taste for more salt and lots of freshly ground pepper. Serves 16.

★*H.F. Pullen*

HADDOCK CHOWDER

Truly a treat at any time, but especially on a cold winter's evening when served with homemade bread or rolls.

2	pounds haddock fillets	2	teaspoons salt
6	medium potatoes	1	teaspoon plus, fines herbes
2	medium onions	1	can evaporated milk butter

Cook potatoes, onions, and fish in water, to cover, for about 20 minutes. Add seasoning. When ready to serve, add 1 can evaporated milk. If too thick, add more evaporated milk. Serve with small pieces of butter in each bowl. Sprinkle with paprika. Serves 6.

★*Margaret Corkum*
★*Bertie Baker*

SHELLFISH GAZPACHO

An excellent lunch for a hot summer day.

2   cups fresh French or Italian breadcrumbs
4   tomatoes, peeled, seeded and chopped
2   cucumbers, peeled and coarsely chopped
1   onion, chopped
1   green pepper, seeded and chopped
2   teaspoons minced fresh garlic
4   cups water
$1/_2$ cup wine vinegar

1   tablespoon salt
    freshly ground pepper
$1/_4$ cup olive oil
1   tablespoon tomato paste
$1^1/_2$ pounds cooked, cleaned shellfish (shrimp, lobster, crab, scallops or combination), chopped or shredded

Garnishes

1   cup croutons
$1/_2$ cup minced onion
$1/_2$ cup peeled, chopped cucumber

$1/_2$ cup minced green pepper
$1/_2$ cup minced fresh parsley
$1/_4$ cup snipped fresh chives

Combine first 6 ingredients in large bowl and blend well. Add water, vinegar, salt and pepper and stir thoroughly. Purée about 2 cups at a time in blender, food processor or food mill. Pour into another large bowl or Dutch oven and slowly whisk in oil and tomato paste. Cover and chill at least 2 hours. Just before serving, add shellfish. Pass garnishes in separate bowls. Serves 6.

★*Mrs. Harold Walker*

To make your chowder lots of fun
Don't forget a dash of rum.

OYSTER AND BRIE CHAMPAGNE SOUP

Sinfully rich, but worth every calorie, this soup is a real party dish.

$^1/_2$ **pound unsalted butter**
$^1/_2$ **cup flour**
2 quarts oyster water or seafood stock (or bottled clam juice)
5 cups whipping cream
$1^1/_2$ **teaspoons red pepper**

$1^1/_2$ **pounds brie cheese, rind removed, cut into small squares**
2 cups dry champagne
3 dozen oysters
1 cup green scallion stems, finely minced
salt, to taste

In 3-quart saucepan, melt butter over low heat, add flour and cook 3 minutes, constantly whisking. Add stock and continue to cook and whisk until flour is absorbed, about 3-4 minutes. Bring to a boil, return to simmer for 10 minutes, whisking occasionally. Add cream, simmer 5 minutes, again whisking constantly. Add red pepper and cheese, whisking until cheese has completely melted. Add oysters and green onions. Cover and let stand for 10 minutes. Taste for seasoning, stir and serve. Serves 8.

★*Alyce Grove*

SEAFOOD CHOWDER

This was served at a church luncheon and was very much enjoyed.

1 can each, clams, lobster shrimp, salmon, crab	3 tablespoons lemon juice
1¹/₂ pounds haddock fillets	1 teaspoon garlic salt
6 diced potatoes	6 cups water
3 cans evaporated milk	2 diced carrots
¹/₂ pound butter	2 diced onions
¹/₂ teaspoon each, salt and pepper	4 tablespoons finely diced fat, salt pork or bacon

Sauté pork or bacon until crisp; remove scraps from pan. Add onion to hot fat and sauté until tender. Add potatoes and water. Simmer about 10 minutes. Add haddock and simmer 10 minutes more. Add all remaining ingredients and simmer, but do not boil. Serves 12.

★Margaret Corkum

TROUT CHOWDER OUT-OF-DOORS

I have often made and eaten this chowder on fishing trips when lunch depended on the morning's catch.

trout	1 teaspoon flour
1¹/₂ cups diced potatoes	1 can evaporated milk
1 onion, thinly sliced	salt and pepper, to taste
2 tablespoons butter	bacon

Cook trout in salted water over an open fire. Skin and bone the fish. For every pound of trout take 1¹/₂ cups diced potatoes and cook potatoes in the water in which you cooked the trout. Fry a thinly sliced onion in 2 tablespoons butter until yellow but not brown; add the flour and cook a moment more. Heat the milk and add the potatoes, onion, trout, salt and pepper. When hot, sprinkle with some crisp crumbled bacon.

★*Marian Straus*

SALT COD SOUP

Good with oatmeal bread.

2 pounds salt cod, soaked in water overnight	$^1/_2$ teaspoon dried thyme
$^1/_2$ cup butter	1 bay leaf
1 onion, sliced	2 tablespoons chopped parsley
4 tomatoes, peeled, seeded and diced	4 potatoes, peeled and sliced
	pepper
2 celery stalks and leaves, chopped	2 cups toasted croutons
2 garlic cloves, crushed	

Drain cod, remove skin and bones, and cut into cubes. Heat butter in a large soup kettle and cook onion and garlic in it for 7 minutes. Add tomatoes, celery and herbs and stir and cook for about 7 minutes longer. Add potatoes and boiling water to cover and simmer for 15 minutes. Add cod and simmer for about 10 minutes longer. Add pepper to taste. Serve the soup with heated bread croutons.

Garlic croutons may be substituted for plain, and ½ cup white wine can be added with the water. Serves 6.

★ *Mrs. Harold Walker*

DUMARESQ OYSTER STEW

This recipe does not appear in any cook-book. It is the result of trial and error — by me, but anyone who has savoured it has found it delicious.

5 or 6 dozen fresh oysters (seems like a lot but oyster stew requires a lot of oysters)
1 can evaporated milk

salt, pepper, and lots of butter
liquor from oysters

Open the oysters; pour the liquid from each into a bowl. Now here comes the tiresome part — wash each oyster in the collected juice until no bit of shell adheres to the oyster; then, strain the juice until no bits of shell, etc., remain in it. I usually line a strainer with cheesecloth (a paper towel will do, but not as well). All you have to do then is put the tin of evaporated milk into a saucepan (on low heat), add the oysters, the juice, salt and pepper to taste, and lots of butter, again to taste. Let this mixture sit on the stove until very hot indeed, but *never* boiling. The longer it sits, the more the beautiful oyster taste permeates the stew. Serve garnished with parsley. Serves 8.

★*Lee Dumaresq*

GORDON'S CHOWDER

The Tabasco and Worcestershire sauces add a touch of piquancy.

1½ pounds haddock fillets	½ cup white wine
5 potatoes	2 cans 2% evaporated milk
5 onions	1 teaspoon butter
2 stalks celery	few drops Tabasco sauce
3 slices bacon	few drops Worcestershire
2½ cups water	sauce
1 bay leaf	salt and pepper, to taste

Cook fish with the bay leaf and wine in the water. Remove all with slotted spoon; flake fish and remove bones. Strain liquid; then to it add cubed potatoes, chopped onion and chopped raw bacon. Cook until done. Add fish and 2 cans milk. Heat and serve. Serves 6.

★ *Sheila M.L. Campbell*

NEW YEAR'S DAY CRABMEAT SOUP

This is very luxurious. I have it for my yearly New Year's Day luncheon. The recipe may be doubled or tripled for however many people you have to feed.

2½ cups chicken bouillon	2 large tablespoons pernod
1 cup chopped onion	1 teaspoon white pepper
2 whole cloves	3 pounds picked over
3 cups whipping cream	crabmeat

Combine bouillon, onion and cloves, and simmer for half an hour. Strain. Return to heat and add cream, pernod and pepper. Heat just to boiling, but do not let it curdle. Pour into a large, deep shell and put crabmeat in a soup bowl and pour steaming hot cream soup over it. Do *not* at any time cook the crabmeat in the soup. It will toughen and not be good. Fresh crabmeat is best, but chopped lobster meat, oysters, or shrimp may be substituted. Serves 6-8.

★*Alyce Grove*

Fixed to the tip of the peninsula
A boot toe curves to fit
The weathered contour of a rugged shore
Where swallows swoop and flit.

And ospreys soar above the lonely pine
Shrill cries of sad lament
Unheeded ebbs the lonely wasteful tide
Hissing its discontent.

CLAM SOUP

A recipe that is simple to prepare and delicious. The minimal clean-up is a real bonus for the busy cook.

3 cups milk	$\frac{1}{2}$ cup heavy cream
2 cups minced clams	salt, freshly ground black
3 tablespoons butter	pepper
	chopped parsley

Heat milk to boiling point, but do not let it burn. Add minced clams, butter, cream and salt and pepper to taste, and heat until the butter has melted and the clams are just hot. Serve in warmed soup bowls, and garnish with parsley. Serves 4.

★*Mrs. Aubrey Smith*

EASY BUT DIVINE-TASTING TOMATO SOUP

You won't find this recipe anywhere else, as it is original.

Simply open a can of Campbell's tomato soup — put this in a blender with half a tin of blend, cream or milk (depending on what kind of a diet you are struggling with). Blend until a nice shade of pink. Slice a *small* onion into paper-thin slices. Put the mixture into a double boiler, add the onion and a generous amount of butter. Serve steaming hot and adorn with greenery.

★*Lee Dumaresq*

GRANDMA'S CHICKEN SOUP

This recipe came to me via my aunt and was made originally by my great grandmother. It is a family favourite, enjoyed by young and old alike.

1	large fat fowl	$1/_4$	cup rice
1	large onion or 2 small	1	egg
1	bay leaf	3	tablespoons flour
6	peppercorns	1	cup cold milk
$1/_2$	teaspoon sage		

Gently boil chicken, onion and spices in enough water to barely cover until very tender. Strain. Boil rice, until soft. Beat until flaky or put through ricer. Add egg to strained rice, beating well together. Bring strained soup to boiling point. Mix flour with milk, being sure that flour has dissolved and mixture is not lumpy. Stir quickly into steaming soup — allowing soup to thicken. Remove soup from heat. Add egg-rice mixture and serve, being careful not to boil soup after egg-rice mixture is added. (The flour-milk mixture can be varied according to thickness desired.) Serves 6.

★*Bertie Baker*

SOUR CREAM OF MUSHROOM SOUP

In Nova Scotia, chanterelles are fairly plentiful in July and August. If you can find some, try them in this soup — absolutely delicious!

$1/_2$	pound mushrooms	1	egg yolk
3	tablespoons butter	1	cup sour cream
1	tablespoon flour	2	tablespoons fresh dill
4	cups chicken or fish bouillon		

Clean and slice large mushrooms. Leave small ones whole. Sauté in butter. Sprinkle with flour. Add bouillon; simmer for 30 to 40 minutes. Beat together the egg yolk, sour cream, and dill. Place in a soup tureen. Pour the hot soup over the cream, stirring constantly. Serves 6.

★*Valda Ondaatje*

SPINACH SOUP

To make a richer soup, add $1/_2$ cup cream.

1	package fresh spinach	2	cans Campbell's chicken broth
1	cup water		
$1/_4$	medium onion	$1/_4$	teaspoon pepper
		4	good shakes nutmeg

Cook spinach in cup of water. Do not overcook — only until tender and still bright green. Chop onion fine. Put spinach and cooking water in blender or food processor with other ingredients. Blend. Serve hot or cold. If hot, add croutons pre-heated in butter in frying pan. Serves 6.

★*Mary T. Grant*

CHANTERELLE SOUP

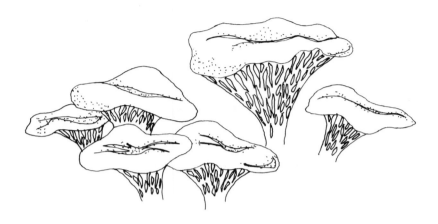

In Nova Scotia there are many kinds of mushrooms. If you are on a walk in the woods and you come across some chanterelles, take them home and try this soup. It's a real delicacy.

4	cups beef stock, made from bones	1	tablespoon butter
2	cups chanterelles, finely chopped	1	tablespoon onion, chopped
1	cup blend milk	1	slice bacon, chopped
1	tablespoon flour		salt, to taste
			pepper, to taste
			parsley

Cook the bacon until crisp and then add the onions and cook until browned. Add the chanterelles and sauté for 5 minutes. Add the hot beef stock and blend cream. Make a thick paste with the flour and the butter and stir in the soup. Simmer for 15 minutes and add salt and pepper to taste. Sprinkle with parsley. Be sure not to wash the mushrooms with water, but use paper towels as to keep all the flavour within the mushrooms. Serves 6.

★*Ilse van de Loo*

MOM'S QUICK-THICK SOUP

Serve with hot tea biscuits — oozing with butter.

$1^1/_2$ to 2 quarts stock, water or gravy, from leftover turkey or chicken dinner
3   chicken bouillon cubes
$1/_4$ cabbage (small), cut into small pieces
$1/_2$ cup diced celery (optional)
$1/_2$ cup long spaghetti (broken into 1-inch pieces)
1   large onion, sliced

salt
pepper
2   cups cooked turkey or chicken
5   canned or cooked tomatoes
$1/_2$ cup cooked wax beans
$1/_2$ cup cooked peas
$1/_2$ cup cooked carrots
1   teaspoon parsley flakes
$1/_2$ cup Minute Rice

In a large pot add stock, water, etc., 1 chicken bouillon cube, the cabbage and celery. Cook until cabbage is almost done and then add broken spaghetti, sliced onion and 2 more bouillon cubes and salt and pepper to taste.

Cook until spaghetti is tender, then add chopped turkey or chicken, tomatoes (quartered), wax beans, peas and carrots.

Bring to boil; add parsley flakes and Minute Rice. Stir well and turn off heat. Cover and let stand $1/_2$ hour before serving. Season to taste. Serves 6.

★*Nina Meisner*

GYPSY HOT SOUP

A 100-year-old family recipe. The fowl or chicken is delicious served cold in sandwiches with this hot soup.

1	large fowl or chicken	1	tablespoon vinegar
	salt and pepper, to taste	2	hot peppers, chopped fine
6	green tomatoes, quartered		cayenne, to taste
6	ripe tomatoes, quartered	6	carrots
6	large onions, quartered	6	potatoes
		6	parsnips

Boil fowl or chicken. When half done (after approximately 60 minutes) add pepper, salt, green and ripe tomatoes, onions, vinegar, hot peppers and cayenne. When almost done, add the rest of the vegetables, quartered. Yield: 6 quarts soup.

★*Mabel B. Lohnes*

CABBAGE CHOWDER

Delicious when made with very fresh vegetables.

4	cups coarsely shredded cabbage	$1/2$	teaspoon sugar
3	cups diced potatoes	$1/2$	teaspoon pepper
2	cups sliced carrots	3	cups water
2	teaspoons salt	4	cups milk
		3	tablespoons butter

Combine the vegetables, seasonings and water. Cook, uncovered, for 10 minutes or until just tender. Add milk and reheat until steaming, then add butter and serve immediately. Serves 8.

★*Leta Udall*

HOTCH-POTCH OR HARVEST BROTH

This soup is only made when the vegetables are at their prime.

2-3 pounds neck of lamb or a   6   young turnips
     beef marrow bone   6   young carrots
$1^1/_2$ pints fresh green peas   6   spring onions
$^1/_2$ pint broad beans   6   sprigs parsley
1   cauliflower $2^1/_2$ quarts water
1   lettuce

Put the neck of the lamb or bone into a pot with cold water and a little salt. Bring to a boil, and skim carefully. Shell peas, shell and skin beans, dice carrots and turnips, peel and chop onions. Retain $^1/_2$ pint of peas; put the rest of prepared vegetables into boiling liquid. Draw to the side and simmer very gently for 3 or 4 hours. It can hardly be cooked too long or too slowly. Half an hour before serving, add the cauliflower in florets, the lettuce, and the rest of the peas. Just before serving, add parsley, finely chopped. The soup should be as thick as porridge and is a meal in itself. Serves 6.

★*Helen Dennis*

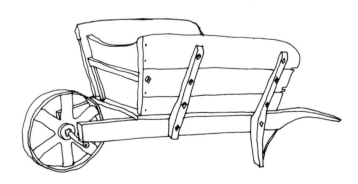

CREAM OF SQUASH SOUP

A must for all squash lovers, and, even if you are not, this soup will convert you.

2	tablespoons grated onion	1	cup heavy cream
2	tablespoons butter		salt
1	package frozen squash thawed, or 2 cups winter squash, cooked and puréed		pepper
			sour cream for garnish (optional)
2	cups chicken broth		

Sauté onion in butter until transparent. Add squash and mix. Stir in chicken broth slowly until well blended. Stir in cream. Cook slowly until thoroughly heated. Season to taste with salt and pepper. Garnish each serving with a dollop of sour cream. Serves 6.

★*Willa Creighton*

CREAM OF CORN SOUP

An easy soup to make, but one with a real homemade flavour.

1	can creamed corn	3	slices onion
1	can water	2	tablespoons butter
1	pint milk	2	tablespoons flour

Empty can of corn into bottom of double boiler. Fill can with water and add to corn over low-medium heat for 20 minutes. Pour milk into top of double boiler with onion slice to simmer while corn is on. Melt butter in small saucepan. Add flour to it, lifting off stove in process. When well mixed, place back on heat and let it bubble, stirring until creamy. When milk is hot, pour it into second mixture, stirring during addition. Remove onion from milk.

Blend the corn mixture in blender and then force through a sieve with a fork. Add some (or all of corn as desired) to give soup body. Mix together corn, water, milk, and cream sauce base. Reheat in double boiler. Serves 6.

★*Nancy E. Kehoe*

Fish and Shellfish

WHITE HEATHER SCALLOPS

The White Heather was a famous Chester racing sloop, renowned for its speed and beauty.

1 pound fresh scallops	$^1/_2$ cup water
flour, to thicken	seafood seasoning, to taste
3 tablespoons butter	

Wash scallops, drain and dry them. Heat 1 tablespoon of the butter in a 10-inch skillet on medium heat. Add scallops and sauté until light brown. Sprinkle with flour. Continue stirring until juice from sautéed scallops thickens. Serve immediately, or scallops will toughen. Serves 4.

★*Bernie "Jake" Freda*

SCALLOPED SCALLOPS

Quick, easy, and delicious.

1 pound fresh scallops	1 pound fresh mushrooms,
1 can cream of celery soup	sliced
	3 tablespoons butter
	buttered crumbs

Parboil scallops for 5 minutes. Sauté mushrooms in 3 tablespoons butter. Place in casserole in layers. Cover with buttered crumbs. Bake for 20 minutes at 325°F. Serves 4.

★*Leith Zinck*

BAKED SCALLOPS

Easy to make and always good. Decorate with a little chopped parsley.

1 pound scallops	2 cups milk
4 tablespoons margarine	$^1/_2$ teaspoon salt
4 tablespoons flour	$^1/_2$ cup buttered crumbs

Place scallops in the bottom of a greased casserole. Melt margarine in the top of a double boiler and stir in flour. Gradually add milk — stirring constantly until sauce thickens. Add salt. Pour sauce over scallops in casserole. Top with buttered crumbs. Bake in an oven at 450°F. for 20 minutes. Serves 4.

★*Mrs. Dale Barkhouse*

SCALLOPS ON THE HALFSHELL

This recipe is fit for a queen!

scallops	Ritz crackers
lobster tails	lemon juice
milk, canned	sherry
butter	

Place scallops on bottoms of half shells. On top of that place some lobster meat. Pour milk over top of fish — just enough to cover. Melt some butter and pour a little on top. Crush some crackers finely and sprinkle on top. Pour a little lemon juice and sherry over all and bake in a 375°F. oven until brown on top.

★*Connie Stevens*

SCALLOPS, BAKED OR BROILED

A recipe that is simple to prepare and delicious.

1 pound scallops	bread crumbs
$1/_4$ pound dry vermouth	lemon wedges
$1/_2$ cup mayonnaise	paprika
$1/_4$ cup margarine	

Melt margarine; add vermouth and mayonnaise; blend over low heat. Place scallops in shallow pan. Cover with sauce and sprinkle with crumbs. Dot with margarine. Sprinkle with paprika. Bake at 400°F. for 15 minutes or broil 6 inches from heat for 10 minutes. Garnish with lemon wedges. Serves 3-4.

★*Cay Armstrong*

CLAM CASSEROLE

Light, good-tasting and good for you!

1 cup crushed crackers	2 eggs, slightly beaten
1 cup milk	$1/_2$ teaspoon salt
1 pint minced clams	$1/_4$ teaspoon pepper

Pour milk over crushed crackers, and let stand for 15 to 20 minutes. Mix pint of minced clams with two slightly beaten eggs, salt and pepper. Alternate layers of crumbs and clams in a greased baking dish. Dot with butter or margarine, and bake 30 to 40 minutes in moderate oven. Serves 4.

★*Leta Udall*

TUNA FISH PIE WITH CHEESE ROLLS

A decorative and delicious dish. Served with a salad, a complete meal.

1/2	cup sliced green pepper		salt
2	slices onion	3	cups milk
3	tablespoons butter	1	large can tuna, drained
6	tablespoons flour	1	tablespoon lemon juice

Melt butter, add green pepper and onion. Cook until soft. Add flour and milk. Stir until smooth and thick. Add remaining ingredients. Pour into a large baking dish and cover with cheese rolls.

Cheese Rolls

1 1/2	cups flour	1/2	cup milk
	salt	3/4	cup grated cheese
	cayenne	2	pimentos, chopped
3	teaspoons baking powder		
3	tablespoons shortening		

Sift first 4 ingredients, add shortening, then milk. Toss on floured board. Roll into sheet 8x2 inches. Sprinkle with cheese and pimento. Roll up like jelly roll. Cut in slices and lay on top of creamed mixture. Bake in a hot oven (450°F), for about 30 minutes.

★*Leith Zinck*

Sugar and spice
And everything nice
Seems needed for cooking delights.
But garlic's a treasure
For true gourmet pleasure
And for raising your love to new heights.

MOULES MARINIÈRE

To prepare the mussels: First, the shells should be tightly closed. Let stand 20 minutes in cold water with 1 tablespoon dry mustard. Scrub thoroughly under running water until all bits of sand have been removed.

1	cup dry white wine	4	dozen mussels, prepared as above
6	shallots, finely chopped, or 3 tablespoons finely chopped onion	2	tablespoons butter salt, if needed few grains cayenne
1	tablespoon chopped parsley		
$1/_2$	bay leaf		

Mix the wine, shallots, parsley, bay leaf and cayenne and let simmer. When reduced to about $1/_2$ cup, strain into a large kettle and add the mussels. Cover tightly. Heat for 5 to 10 minutes, or until the shells open, shaking the pan from time to time. Remove the mussels carefully to deep soup plates and keep hot.

To sauce in the kettle add butter and salt, if necessary. Pour carefully over the mussels, leaving any sediment in the bottom of the pan. Sprinkle with parsley. Serves 6.

★*Clarissa Gibbs*

SUPERB MUSSELS AND CLAMS

A quick delicious meal.

mussels
clams
cooking oil
lemon

potatoes, cooked
lettuce leaves
cucumbers

Fry mussels and clams in oil until tender. Drain on paper towel. Place on serving dishes and decorate with fried potatoes, lettuce leaves, cucumbers or any other greens on hand.

★*Connie Stevens*

LOBSTER NEWBURG

A wonderful party dish. Pastry cases make a very festive-looking presentation.

$1/_3$ cup butter or margarine
2 tablespoons all purpose flour
2 cups light cream
4 beaten egg yolks
$1/_2$ teaspoon salt

2 5-ounce cans lobster, or 12 ounces of fresh lobster
$1/_4$ cup cooking sherry
2 teaspoons lemon juice
toast points or
pastry cups
paprika

Melt butter in chafing dish or skillet. Blend in flour and gradually stir in cream. Cook slowly, stirring constantly until thick. Stir small amounts of sauce into egg yolks and return to hot mixture. Cook until blended, stirring constantly for about 1 minute (don't overcook). Add lobster, cooking sherry, lemon juice and salt. Heat through. Serve over toast points or in pastry cups. Sprinkle with paprika. Serves 6.

★*Hilda Tzagarakis*

DRUNKEN WHITEGATE LOBSTER

This is a very special dish. It's no good getting the tiny one, or two, or even three-pound lobsters that everyone gets for a lobster feast. For this very special feast you have to have one of the large ten to twenty-pound kings of the sea. Lobsters are erotic, sensuous, and contain the phosphorus that will increase your vigor and stem your ebbing tide. You will find that this sumptuous meal will indeed raise your stature.

1	10-pound lobster		raw garlic
3	bay leaves		cold water
4	glasses of white French burgundy wine	1	large lobster-steaming cauldron

Immerse the lobster in top of the large lobster steaming cauldron, put cold water in the bottom, and gently bring the water to a boil. Be careful not to immerse the lobster in boiling water as he won't be nearly as tasty. When the water is hot add the four glasses of white wine to the cauldron, also the bay leaves and garlic. The wine should make the lobster quite tipsy, and you will have to let him steam in his cauldron for about one hour, by which time he will be ready for eating. Fabulous with baked potatoes, garlic bread, and Caesar salad.

★ *Christopher Ondaatje*

LOBSTER TAILS IN BUTTERED RUM —
A Victory Feast for the Crew of The Ripple

There is an old Chester story that God sprinkled the waters of Mahone Bay with aphrodisiacs because he could not stand to see desire thwarted by inactivity.

Take a handful of these aphrodisiacs or lobster tails and you can let your own performance be your guide! Both the lobster and the rum are powerful and potent — and if you doubt the validity of this boast, ask any crew member of the Ripple.

5 lobster tails	1 tablespoon chopped parsley
5 cloves chopped garlic	$^1/_4$ cup butter
2 cups black rum	white salt and black pepper
2 teaspoons lemon juice	

Once you have removed the lobster from its shell, cut it into chunks. Melt the butter, add the lemon juice, garlic, and then add the parsley, salt, and butter. Mix well, and only add the black rum just before you immerse the lobster meat in your brew. Sauté briefly and serve.

★ *Christopher Ondaatje*

LOBSTER CASSEROLE

Simple to make, but wonderful tasting.

2	small onions	2	eggs
$1/_2$	pound fresh mushrooms	$1^1/_2$	cups milk
	butter	2	cups lobster meat
3	tablespoons flour		bread crumbs

Sauté onions and fresh mushrooms in butter for 3 minutes. Add flour. Beat eggs with milk and add to onions and mushrooms. Then add cut up lobster. Top with bread crumbs and bake 10 minutes at 450°F.

★*Elaine Heisler*

SWORDFISH STEAKS WITH LEMON AND CAPERS

Delicious when made with very fresh swordfish. This recipe also works well with halibut steaks. Serve with spinach purée and new potatoes.

3 to 4	lemons	12	tablespoons oil
6	slices swordfish (about 8 ounces each)	1	teaspoon butter
		5	tablespoons unsalted butter
	salt and white pepper	$1/_4$	cup drained capers
	milk	2	tablespoons chopped fresh parsley (garnish)
	all-purpose flour		

Carefully peel lemons, discarding all of white pith. Cut white membrane from lemon sections. Remove segments, then dice.

Generously season swordfish with salt and white pepper. Dip each slice in milk. Coat with flour, shaking off excess.

Heat 6 tablespoons oil in large skillet over medium-high heat. Stir in $^1/_2$ teaspoon butter. Add 3 slices of fish and sauté until lightly browned on both sides. Reduce heat and continue cooking until fish is opaque and feels firm to touch. Transfer to heated serving platter and keep warm. Repeat with remaining oil, $^1/_2$ teaspoon butter, and fish.

Wipe out skillet. Add remaining 5 tablespoons butter and cook over medium heat until foaming; add capers and lemon slices. Heat until all is hot, then pour over swordfish, garnish with parsley and serve at once. Serves 6.

★*Valda Ondaatje*

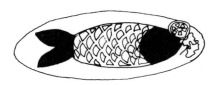

CHESTER SWORDFISH

This is, by far, my favourite recipe for swordfish — a firm-fleshed, almost meaty fish and a great delicacy.

	swordfish steak, 1 to 1½ inches thick	3	tablespoons butter
	salt, to taste	3	tablespoons Worcestershire sauce
3	tablespoons lemon juice	1	cup sour cream

Wipe swordfish steak with paper towel. Place on oven rack and broil for 5 minutes. Remove from oven and spread thickly with sour cream. Sprinkle with salt and return to 425 F. oven. Bake for approximately 20 minutes, or, until just done. Mix lemon juice, butter, and Worcestershire sauce and pour into sauceboat to serve with fish. Serves 4.

★*Deborah Grant*

COLD SALMON WITH WATERCRESS MOUSSELINE

An elegant way of serving cold salmon, but be careful not to overcook it, or it will be dry and lacking in flavour. The salmon should be moist and redolent of the herbs it was cooked in.

4	fresh salmon steaks	
2	cups water	
$^1/_2$	onion, sliced	
1	stalk celery, sliced	
1	bay leaf	
	juice of 1 lemon	
	salt and pepper	

Watercress Mousseline

2	bunches watercress
$^3/_4$	cup whipping cream
	salt and pepper
	juice of $^1/_2$ lemon

Combine water, onion, celery, bay leaf, lemon juice, salt and pepper to taste, in a wide saucepan. Bring to boil, reduce heat and simmer for 15 minutes. Add salmon steaks to simmering liquid; do not let them overlap. Cover and simmer for 10 minutes, or until cooked. Chill steaks in the liquid. Just before serving, drain. Arrange on a bed of lettuce and put watercress mousseline sauce in the hole found in each salmon steak. Decorate with sprigs of watercress. Serves 4.

Watercress Mousseline
Remove leaves from watercress stalks. Place them in water and simmer for 10 minutes. Bring cream to a boil, add sieved watercress and season. Chill. Just before serving beat in lemon juice until sauce is thick and smooth.

★ *Valda Ondaatje*

When cooking lobster in a pot
Make sure the water's warm — not hot.
Then bring it slowly to a boil
Or else the lobster's taste will spoil.

BAKED HALIBUT

Tangy and tender, this dish makes its own sauce.

3 to 4 pounds halibut steaks	**butter**
$1/_4$ cup white wine	**sea salt**
juice of $1/_2$ lemon	**fines herbes**

Place fish flat in baking pan and pour wine and lemon over it. Dot all over with butter and sprinkle lightly with sea salt and fines herbes. Bake at 375°F. for about 35 minutes. Serves 6.

★*Bertie Baker*

OVEN-FRIED HADDOCK A LA NIÇOISE

All but the final cooking can be done well ahead of time.

2	**pounds haddock fillets**	**2**	**cloves garlic, finely chopped**
1	**tablespoon salt**		**freshly grated peel of $1/_2$**
1	**cup milk**		**lemon**
1	**cup breadcrumbs**	**$1/_4$**	**teaspoon thyme**
2-4	**tablespoons parsley, finely chopped**	**4**	**tablespoons melted butter**
			lemon wedges

Pre-heat oven to 450°F. Add salt to the milk. Dip fillets in the milk, and then in the breadcrumbs, which have been mixed with finely chopped parsley and garlic, grated lemon peel and thyme. Arrange fish pieces in a well-buttered baking dish and pour the melted butter over them. Bake in the top half of the oven for about 12 minutes. Serve with lemon wedges. Serves 4-6.

★*Mrs. John Fraser*

FRESH FISH FILLET CASSEROLE

Great with a spinach salad and warm bread.

1½ pounds fresh fish fillets
    dash garlic
    lemon juice
    salt and pepper, to taste

1 can condensed cream of
    mushroom soup
    grated cheese
    cracker crumbs
    butter

Fry fillets, seasoned with garlic and lemon, in lots of butter. When flaky, put in a casserole and pour mushroom soup over top of fish and then add grated cheese. Sprinkle cracker crumbs on and then a little melted butter. Cook in a 350°F. oven until soup is boiling and crumbs and cheese are brown.

★*Connie Stevens*

HADDOCK CASSEROLE

All but the final cooking can be done ahead of time.

2   pounds haddock
1   cup bread crumbs
¹/₄ cup onion
1   10-ounce can mushrooms
    or fresh mushrooms

¹/₄ cup butter
¹/₄ teaspoon savory
¹/₄ teaspoon salt
1   egg, beaten
1   can mushroom soup

Melt butter. Add onion and mushrooms. Cook for 5 minutes. Add salt and savory to bread crumbs and blend. Add bread crumb mixture to beaten eggs. Place half of the fish in a casserole. Then add crumbs, the rest of the fish and the can of soup. Cook in a 325°F. oven for 25 - 30 minutes. Serves 6.

★*Hilda Tzagarakis*

CHESTER FISH BUBBLY

Simple, and very, very good.

2	pounds fresh haddock or cod fillets	2	tablespoons chopped green pepper
1	can mushroom soup		salt and pepper
1	tablespoon lemon juice	1	cup grated cheese
2	tablespoons minced onion		

Cut fillets into 8 serving pieces. Place in buttered, rectangular casserole. Mix soup, lemon juice, onion, green pepper, salt and pepper and pour over fillet pieces. Top with grated cheese. Bake 20-25 minutes at 400°F. until bubbling. Serve immediately. Serves 6-8.

★*Peggy McAlpine*

MICROWAVE FISH FILLETS

Evie Taylor Searle gave me this recipe when we first moved to Chester, and I have found it invaluable ever since.

butter	bread crumbs, seasoned
fillets	paprika
mayonnaise	

Butter dish. Cover both sides of the fillets with mayonnaise. Sprinkle with seasoned crumbs on both sides. Place in a dish and sprinkle with paprika. Cover with Saran Wrap and cook on high temperature for approximately 6 minutes per pound.

★*Gail Fraser*

BAKED FISH FOR 4

Serve with peas and rice. A meal fit for a king!

1	2- or 3-pound haddock		pepper, to taste
1	green pepper	2	tablespoons mayonnaise
1	apple		butter
	salt, to taste	½	small onion (optional)

Put haddock in a baking dish with ½ cup water and spread mayonnaise over top of the fish. Put in a 375°F. oven for 30 minutes. Do *not* preheat the oven. Meanwhile, slice the green pepper into ¹/₄-inch strips and then cut those in half. Cut an apple into quarters -- take the core out but do not peel it. Take the fish out of the oven, place the apple around it and sprinkle the green pepper on as well. Put back in oven for 15 more minutes. Serves 4.

★*Butch Heisler*

SOUTH SHORE FISH BAKE

A different dish each time you use a different soup for the sauce.

1 package frozen fish fillets, partially thawed and cut into 4 portions	1 teaspoon grated onion
	$^1/_4$ cup milk
	pepper, to taste
10- ounce can of celery, tomato or mushroom soup	$^1/_4$ cup grated Cheddar cheese (optional)

Preheat oven to 450°F. In a saucepan combine soup, onion, milk and pepper. Cover and simmer over low heat for 5 minutes, stirring occasionally. Meanwhile, place fillets in a greased casserole dish. Pour sauce over fish. For a variation, top with grated cheese. Bake for 30 minutes or until fish flakes easily. Serves 4.

★*Connie Stevens*

TROUT FISHCAKES

This recipe for trout fishcakes comes from one of two cookbooks written by my mother-in-law, Gladys Straus, for her children and friends.

$^1/_2$ cup cooked, boned, skinned trout	yolk of one egg
	salt and pepper, to taste
2 tablespoons mashed potatoes	freshly cut chives
2 tablespoons butter	

Combine. Pat into cakes and fry in one tablespoon butter. Serves 1.

★*Marian Straus*

MRS. EISNOR'S HADDOCK FILLETS

This is easy to prepare and very good. It is the recipe of Charlotte Eisnor, who has been serving us delicious meals for twenty-six years. Whenever possible we buy fresh haddock with no preservatives. It is far superior, and we are often able to get this in Chester.

1$^1/_2$pounds haddock fillets	salt
$^1/_2$ cup crushed cornflakes	pepper
$^1/_4$ cup melted butter	

Cut fillet in serving size pieces and place in shallow baking dish. Use enough milk to almost cover fish. Season with salt and pepper. Put fish in 300°F. oven and bake for about 20 minutes or just until fish flakes. Cover with crushed cornflakes, drizzle with melted butter and put back in oven until ready to serve—10 or so minutes. Serves 4.

★Helen Bethune

FISH FILLETS IN BATTER

Tastes best with very fresh fish — haddock, halibut or sole.

1 cup sifted all-purpose flour	1 tablespoon softened butter
$^1/_2$ teaspoon salt	1 egg, slightly beaten
dash of pepper	fish fillets
1 cup milk	

Cut fillets into serving pieces. Sift together flour, salt and pepper. Slightly beat egg, with beater, add the milk and margarine. Mix until light. Pour in flour and beat until smooth. Dip fish into batter before frying in very hot fat.

★Connie Stevens

HADDOCK DELIGHT

Good for any occasion, and especially good if fish is freshly caught. Any fish fillets may be substituted for the haddock.

2 pounds haddock fillets salt and freshly ground pepper, in moderation fines herbes butter	$^1/_2$ package frozen mushrooms or $^1/_2$ pound fresh, if available 1 cup grated farmer's cheese paprika parsley

Place fish fillets in buttered, shallow baking pan. Season lightly with salt and pepper. Sprinkle generously with fines herbes. Dot with butter. Over top place mushrooms, and over all the grated cheese. Bake in 375°F. oven for about 35 minutes. Decorate with paprika and parsley.

★*Bertie Baker*

ACADIAN FISH DINNER

A traditional Nova Scotian dish — fish and vegetables in one dish.

1 pound haddock fillets	1 garlic clove, minced
$^1/_4$ cup butter	1 tablespoon flour
3 cups thinly sliced potatoes	1 teaspoon salt
1$^1/_2$ cups thinly sliced carrots	$^3/_4$ cup milk, warmed 1 tablespoon cooking oil

Preheat oven to 350°F. Melt butter in a large saucepan and sauté onions until tender. Add potatoes, carrots, garlic and stir-fry for 5 minutes, stirring constantly. Sprinkle with flour and salt, stir to coat well. Add milk and heat until bubbly. Spoon into 2-quart greased casserole dish. Cover. Bake 30 minutes or until potatoes are nearly done. Uncover. Arrange fillets on potato mixture. Brush fillets with oil. Cover and bake an additional 25 to 30 minutes. Serves 4.

★*Connie Stevens*

When frying scallops in a pan
Add some salt and marjoram.

HADDOCK PARMIGIANA

A wonderful fish casserole that can be prepared ahead of time and baked just before serving.

1$^1/_2$ **pounds haddock fillets**	$^1/_2$ **teaspoon basil**
$^1/_4$ **cup diced bread crumbs**	1 **jar spaghetti sauce**
$^3/_4$ **teaspoon garlic salt**	1 **8-ounce package mozzarella**
3 **tablespoons butter**	**cheese, grated**
1 **medium onion, finely**	1 **8-ounce package egg**
chopped	**noodles**
$^1/_4$ **cup mushrooms, finely**	
chopped	

Cut fish into equal pieces. Combine crumbs and garlic salt and coat fish. Set aside. Melt butter, add onion and sauté until soft. Add mushrooms and basil. Sauté for 1 minute longer. Stir in spaghetti sauce and remove from heat. Spoon $^1/_2$ cup sauce into 9-inch square pan and place fish on top. Spoon remaining sauce over fish and sprinkle with mozzarella cheese. Cover with foil and bake in a 425°F. oven for 20 minutes. Remove foil and bake for 2 to 3 minutes. Cook egg noodles and drain. Place fish and sauce over noodles. Serves 4.

★*Thirsty Thinkers Tea Room*

HADDOCK IN APPLE CIDER

It is well known in Nova Scotia that crab apples are used to keep your skin from wrinkling and to give you strength for sexual encounters. (Some Maritime doctors still prescribe apple feasting to acquire rejuvenation.)

2 pound haddock	**1 pint apple cider**
1$^1/_2$ dozen clams	**parsley**

Place your haddock gently in a greased baking pan, and cover the fish with a layer of clams. Pour the cider into the pan until it just covers the fish. Bake in a 350°F. oven until the fish is tender and the cider is reduced to about half its volume.

Be careful your dish is not overdone.

Serve with mushrooms.

★*Christopher Ondaatje*

TUNA CASSEROLE

In a time of rising food prices, here's a welcome meal indeed!

1 small tin tuna	**1 small tin mushroom soup**
1 bag potato chips	

Crush potato chips and put in the casserole dish. Add tuna and cover with mushroom soup. Bake in a 350°F. for $^1/_2$ hour. Serves 4.

★*Margaret Pulsifer*

FISH DISH

A very decorative dish for a special occasion.

$^1/_4$ cup finely chopped onion
$^1/_3$ cup corn oil
3 cups soft bread crumbs
$^1/_2$ cup hot milk
2 tablespoons chopped parsley
$^3/_4$ teaspoon salt

$^1/_4$ teaspoon pepper
$^1/_4$ teaspoon savory
2 pounds fish (sole, haddock, perch)
3 tablespoons corn oil
$1^1/_2$ tablespoons lemon juice

Sauté onion in oil. Add crumbs, milk, parsley, salt, pepper and savory. Mix well. Place fillets around inside of large greased muffin tins. Fill centre with stuffing. Brush tops with oil and lemon juice - mixed. Bake in a 375°F. oven for 25 minutes. Brush occasionally with oil-lemon mixture. Lift out of pans while hot. Garnish with paprika and parsley. Serves 8.

★*Leith Zinck*

TUNA FISH AND MACARONI CASSEROLE

Easy and economical — a great lunch or Sunday night supper dish.

1	cup cooked macaroni	1	can tuna
3	tablespoons margarine or butter	$^1/_2$	cup chopped onion
2	tablespoons flour	$^1/_2$	cup chopped green pepper
$1^1/_4$	cups milk		salt, to taste
1	can cream of chicken soup		pepper, to taste
			bread crumbs
			grated cheese

Cook macaroni. Sauté onions and green pepper until the onions are just golden brown. Add flour and blend. Add milk and stir until thickened. Stir in soup and tuna. Put in a greased casserole covered with bread crumbs and grated cheese. Bake at 350°F. for 30 - 45 minutes. Serves 4.

★*Hilda Tzagarakis*

DUTCHMAN'S SPECIAL

A traditional Nova Scotia favourite.

1	pound salted codfish	2	pounds fresh pork
2	large onions		

Soak codfish for 3 to 4 hours, then put on top of stove in cold water and bring just to a boil, then drain. Do this 3 or 4 times. Cut into pieces. Cut pork into very fine pieces and fry until brown. Cut onions small and add to pork and fry. Add to codfish. Season with pepper and serve with seasonal vegetables. Serves 6.

★*Leta Udall*

Poultry

CHICKEN WITH BEER AND MAPLE SYRUP

An invention of mine. The slight bitterness of the beer and the sweetness of the maple syrup make an interesting contrast.

2	tablespoons olive oil	$^1/_3$	cup maple syrup
2 or 3	garlic cloves, chopped		Italian seasoning
1	cup onions, coarsely chopped		bay leaf
			grated nutmeg
$^1/_2$	cup green pepper	1	chicken, cut up and
$^1/_4$	can tomato paste		skinned
$^3/_4$	can beer		

Sauté onions, garlic and green pepper in oil until soft and cooked. Add tomato paste, beer and maple syrup and cook for 5 minutes. Add seasonings and chicken, cut into 2 legs and second joints and two breasts, and simmer until chicken is tender. Serves 4 or 5.

★Eleanor Seyffert

BRANDIED CHICKEN BREASTS

This is my favourite chicken recipe, with which I part rather regretfully. However, it is for a very worthy cause.

8	chicken breasts, boned and skinned	2	cups light cream
	brandy		nutmeg
	salt, pepper, thyme	$^1/_2$	cup Swiss cheese, grated
3	tablespoons butter	$^1/_2$	cup buttered bread crumbs
$^1/_2$	cup sherry		

Sprinkle a little brandy over chicken breasts and let stand 10 minutes. Season with salt, pepper and thyme. Melt butter and sauté chicken breasts on both sides just until firm (4 or 5 minutes on each side). Remove to a heated platter and keep warm. To remaining butter and pan juices, add sherry and simmer until liquid is reduced by half. Add cream, season with salt, pepper and nutmeg and cook until slightly thickened. Pour sauce over chicken breasts. Sprinkle with grated cheese and bread crumbs mixed together and glaze under broiler. Serves 8.

★*Valda Ondaatje*

MADAME PANDIT'S GINGERED CHICKEN

The yogurt will form a crust over a subtle, tantalizing flavour.

chicken breasts, thighs or legs **melted butter**	**powdered ginger** **unflavoured yogurt**

Brush chicken parts lightly with butter and spread with powdered ginger. (Do not rub in. Spread with knife, using more or less ginger, according to taste. A light touch is recommended the first time.) Then, over the ginger, spread a lavish coat of yogurt. Allow to marinate for at least two hours or overnight in the refrigerator. Bake in a 350°F. oven for 1 hour.

Note: the same method may be used with a roasting chicken. Allow $^3/_4$ hour more time for baking.

★Cay Armstrong

BARBECUED CHICKEN

Roll pieces of chicken in flour with salt and pepper; while chicken is browning in butter, make the following sauce:

1 **medium onion, cut into small pieces**	1 **teaspoon white sugar**
1 **teaspoon garlic powder**	1 **tablespoon brown sugar**
1 **teaspoon salt**	1 **tablespoon Worcestershire Sauce**
$^1/_4$ **teaspoon pepper**	$^1/_4$ **cup vinegar**
$^1/_4$ **teaspoon dry mustard**	$1^1/_2$ **cups tomato juice or**
2 **bay leaves**	**V8 juice**

Mix and pour over chicken. Simmer until chicken is tender.

★Kathleen Rowan-Legg

CHICKEN SAUCE

Served with rice and a salad, an easy-to-prepare and delicious meal.

1 chicken	3 tablespoons lemon juice
1 cup water	2 tablespoons cornstarch
$1/_2$ cup brown sugar	$1/_2$ teaspoon ginger
$1/_2$ cup ketchup	$1/_2$ teaspoon tumeric
$1/_4$ cup vinegar	1 garlic clove, mashed

Cook chicken until it is half done, combine the other ingredients and pour over chicken. Bake until done. Serves 4.

★*Shirley Moody*

You shake and shake the ketchup bottle
None will come — and then a lot'll.

HONEYED CHICKEN

This is one of our favourite dishes. Very easy, very good, and frequently requested by young people.

1 frying chicken, cut into serving pieces	$1/_4$ cup prepared mustard
$1/_2$ cup liquid honey	2 teaspoons curry powder

Put chicken in baking pan. Combine honey, mustard and curry powder. Pour honey mixture over chicken. Bake, covered, for 45 minutes in a 350°F. oven. Uncover. Bake another 20 to 30 minutes until pleasantly brown. Serve with rice or noodles.

★*Bertie Baker*

CHICKEN VEGETABLE STEW

A wonderful old-fashioned stew, full of flavour and goodness.

2 pints homemade chicken broth
$^1/_2$ cup alphabet noodles
4 carrots
$^1/_2$ cup celery
1 large tomato
$^1/_3$ cup fresh green beans vege-salt, to taste

1 cup cream sauce, made with 2 tablespoons butter and flour and 1 cup evaporated milk
1 large Gravenstein apple
$^1/_2$ chicken breast from large (6-pound) roasting chicken

Combine above ingredients (except cream sauce), carefully diced in small pieces, and cook until vegetables are tender. Add cream sauce. Serves 4.

★*Olive G. Dorey*

CHICKEN BROTH

Use for Chicken Vegetable Stew, above.

6 pound chicken
3 quarts water
3 stalks celery
1 bay leaf

1 medium onion
6 stems parsley
6 cloves
2 carrots

Combine ingredients and cook for 4 hours. Strain. Cool and skim. Makes 5 pints broth. (Add 6 peppercorns if desired, and salt to taste.)

★*Bertie Baker*

TURKEY BREAST SCALLOPINE

This dish can be made with veal, as in the traditional recipe, but turkey breast meat is much less expensive, and, if not overdone, just as tender.

12 turkey cutlets, about $^3/_8$ inch thick	12 thin slices ham
$^1/_2$ cup flour	1 cup sautéed sliced mushrooms
12 tablespoons ($1^1/_2$ sticks) butter	$^1/_2$ cup grated Parmesan cheese
6 tablespoons oil	$^1/_2$ cup chicken or turkey broth
salt, freshly ground black pepper	chopped parsley

Pound the cutlets lightly between sheets of waxed paper until thin. Flour the slices lightly.

Use 2 skillets for sautéing so the pan will not be overcrowded. Melt half the butter with half the oil in each skillet. When hot, add the turkey slices and sauté quickly, turning them once and seasoning with salt and pepper as they cook. You will probably have to do this in 2 or 3 batches. Do not overcook. Put a slice of ham on each cutlet and spoon some of the mushrooms on top. Sprinkle with the Parmesan cheese, add the broth, cover and simmer for about 5 minutes, or until the cheese has melted.

Arrange turkey on a hot platter and spoon the pan juices over the top. Sprinkle with chopped parsley. Serves 6.

★Mrs. W.W. Ogilvie

FRANK THE PIRATE'S WIFE'S CHICKEN

Out of the ordinary and very good.

1 large chicken, cut into 8 pieces	tarragon
	ginger
$1/_4$ cup cornflakes	salt and pepper
2 tablespoons sunflower seeds	saffron
	lemon
2 tablespoons toasted sesame seeds	parsley
$1/_4$ cup rolled oats	
1 garlic clove, minced oregano	

Blend cornflakes, put in plastic bag with seeds, oats, garlic, oregano, tarragon, ginger, salt and pepper, all to taste, and shake pieces of chicken in it. Put on baking sheet and bake at 375°F. for 1 hour. Garnish with lemon and parsley. Serves 4.

★Eleanor Seyffert

COQ-AU-VIN

A fairly easy coq-au-vin recipe, it is nevertheless chock full of flavour. Smoky back bacon adds extra flavour.

4   chicken legs
3   slices bacon, diced
2   tablespoons cooking oil
12 button onions
12 mushroom caps
    salt and pepper, to taste
    flour
2   cloves garlic, chopped
2   bay leaves

$^1/_2$ teaspoon thyme
2   sprigs parsley
4   tablespoons brandy, warmed
$^1/_2$ bottle red wine
1   teaspoon sugar
1   tablespoon flour
1   tablespoon butter
3   tablespoons parsley, chopped

Remove skin from chicken legs and separate into drumsticks and thighs. In a heatproof casserole, slightly sauté bacon in oil, add onions; cook for a minute or two, then add mushrooms. Sauté gently until onions are transparent; remove from casserole. Roll chicken pieces in seasoned flour and sauté in same fat for about 5 minutes or until golden. Return onions, mushrooms, bacon to casserole. Add salt, pepper, garlic, thyme, bay leaves and parsley; cover and cook in a 350°F. oven until almost tender (about 25 minutes). Transfer chicken, bacon and vegetables to a clean casserole and keep warm. Skim off excess fat from pan juices; bring to a boil, add warmed brandy and ignite. Allow to burn for a minute or two and then extinguish by pouring in wine. Add sugar, bring to boil and reduce sauce to half the original quantity. Thicken with a *beurre manie* made of a tablespoon each flour and butter. Strain sauce over chicken and vegetables; cover and simmer in a very slow oven until ready to serve. Garnish with chopped parsley. Serves 4.

★*Valda Ondaatje*

LIBBY'S CHICKEN DIVAN

The sauce makes this Chicken Divan outstanding. Serve with rice and a green salad. For garnish, cherry tomatoes add colour.

3	large chicken breasts, split, boned, and cooked	$3/_4$	cup mayonnaise
3	boxes frozen broccoli (fresh is better)	2	teaspoons Worcestershire Sauce
3	tablespoons butter	$1/_2$	teaspoon nutmeg
3	tablespoons flour	$4^1/_2$	tablespoons sherry
$1^1/_2$	cups milk	$3/_4$	cup heavy cream, whipped
1	can cream of celery soup	$3/_4$	cup buttered bread crumbs
		1	cup Parmesan cheese

Cook chicken breasts as you wish. (Roasting in butter preserves the moist flavour.) Cook broccoli until just tender. Make cream sauce of butter, flour, milk. Add soup, mayonnaise, Worcestershire Sauce and nutmeg. Mix well. Add sherry. Add whipped cream just before pouring over chicken.

Put chicken in large, flat casserole; arrange broccoli on top and pour sauce over all. Cover with a thin layer of bread crumbs and lots of Parmesan cheese. Bake at 325°F. for approximately 25 minutes, until heated through, but not bubbling. Do not overcook. Serves 6.

★Elizabeth Frise

Oh hummingbirds of Chester
You have no hum, of course
But who knows by what magic
You hold your winged course.

Deep into the petal's curve
Sweet feast of life bloodgold
What secret does your tongue confess
Of beauty still untold?

QUICK CHICKEN PIE

For the cook in a hurry.

1 can cream of chicken soup
2 cups cooked chicken (cut into bite-sized pieces)
1 cup cooked carrots
1 cup cooked peas
salt and pepper, to taste
pastry for one-crust pie

Combine all ingredients (except pastry) and pour into a greased baking dish. Cover with pastry and bake at 350°F. until crust is golden brown (about 30 minutes). Serves 6.

Crust

1$^1/_2$ cups flour
$^1/_2$ cup shortening
scant teaspoon salt
$^1/_4$ cup milk (approximately)

Mix flour, shortening and salt with pastry blender. Add enough milk to roll out easily.

★*Nina Meisner*

BARBECUED CHICKEN WINGS

A delicious, low-cost dinner when served with rice and sautéed mushrooms and green peppers.

2 pounds chicken wings
$^2/_3$ cup brown sugar
4 tablespoons vinegar
4 tablespoons soy sauce
salt and pepper, to taste
garlic powder
2 chicken bouillon cubes

Split joints of chicken wings; flour them and brown in a little fat. Lay them flat (the flatter the better) in a baking dish. For each pound of chicken crumble across the top $^1/_3$ cup of brown sugar, over that sprinkle 2 tablespoons vinegar and 2 tablespoons soy sauce, a little garlic powder, and a cube of chicken bouillon crumbled across the top. Add salt and pepper to taste. Put a cover on the dish and bake at 325°F. for 45 minutes. Serves 4 to 6.

★ *Elizabeth Pellow*

CRISPY DUCK HUNAN STYLE

For enthusiasts of crisp duck, this tops all. Serve Chinese style by cutting duck into bite-sized squares with a cleaver.

1   4¹/₂-to 5-pound duck

Marinade

6	slices peeled fresh ginger		broth, stock or water
5	green onions	1	tablespoon soy sauce
3	tablespoons salt		peanut oil
1	tablespoon rice wine or dry Sherry	1	teaspoon freshly ground pepper
¹/₂	star anise		

Prick duck all over.

Pulverize ingredients for marinade in blender. Rub over duck inside and out. Let duck stand at room temperature for 30 minutes to absorb flavours.

Steam over broth, stock or water for 1 hour. Remove and let cool slightly. Carefully pat dry, then rub skin with soy sauce.

Pour about 3 inches oil in Dutch oven and heat to 400°F. Carefully lower duck breast side up into oil. Cover and fry 10 minutes. Turn breast side down and fry 10 minutes longer. Remove with large tongs and let excess oil drain off. Cut into small squares and serve. Serves 4.

★ *Eleanor Seyffert*

ROAST DUCK

I like this served on a bed of stewed kraut; however, rice may appeal more to others.

Stuffing

1¹/₂	onions	1	teaspoon caraway seeds
2	apples	1	teaspoon juniper berries
2	cups sauerkraut, rinsed and drained	¹/₂	cup dry vermouth
	butter		salt and pepper, to taste

Sauté onions and apples in butter. Add the sauerkraut, caraway seeds, juniper berries, vermouth, salt and pepper. Simmer until blended. (If using raw kraut, cook it first).

Duck

Stuff the duck and season skin with salt and pepper. Bake in a 325°F. oven for 2 hours.

Sauce

2	tablespoons brown sugar	2	tablespoons duck drippings
1	tablespoon cornstarch	3	tablespoons orange liqueur
1	tablespoon grated orange peel		giblet stock, to thin
²/₃	cup orange juice		

Dissolve cornstarch in orange juice and combine with rest of ingredients. Heat.

★*Gail Fraser*

Meat

JAMBALAYA

Eternity, they say, is a ham and two people. Here's a good way of using up some of that leftover ham.

3	tablespoons oil	$1/_2$	cup Scotch whiskey
1	cup onion, finely chopped	$1/_2$	teaspoon basil
2	cloves garlic, pressed	$1/_4$	teaspoon marjoram
2	cups diced, cooked ham	$1/_4$	teaspoon thyme
1	cup celery in $1/_2$ inch pieces	$1/_2$	teaspoon pepper
		1	teaspoon paprika
1	8-ounce can tomato sauce	1	cup raw rice (Carolina long grain)
1	$10^1/_2$ ounce can beef broth		
1	cup water	$1/_2$	pound cooked shrimp, or 2 4-ounce cans tiny shrimp

Heat oil in a large casserole that can also be used on top of stove. Cook onion and garlic until soft. Add all remaining ingredients except rice and shrimp and bring to a boil. Slowly add rice, return to a boil; cover and reduce heat. Simmer for 20 minutes or until rice is almost done. Add shrimp, cover and cook 5 minutes longer. Serves 6.

★*Sally Farrell*

OVEN-BAKED PORK CHOPS

I like doing my pork chops this way; pork requires a little more cooking than other meat, but it is tender and juicy.

4	pork chops, or as many as required	1	chopped onion
1	can of mushroom or celery soup		dash of garlic, pepper, and salt to taste (not too much salt, as the soup is salted)
1	can of water		

Sear pork chops in frying pan; place in covered casserole; add chopped onion and seasoning. Add 1 can of mushroom or celery soup and 1 can of water. Cover; cook in 350°F. oven for 1 hour. Serve with mashed turnip and baked potatoes.

★*Mrs. Cavell Stevens*

DRESSED PORK CHOPS

Here is a dinner that can wait to be served.

3-4 pounds thick loin pork chops

Place bread dressing between chops. Tie together with string and bake fat side up at 325°F. for 2 to 3 hours.

Bread Dressing:

2	cups white bread, crumbled	1	tablespoon Tancook summer savory
1	large onion, chopped		salt and pepper

When baked, place on platter. Remove string. Garnish with parsley and small browned potatoes. Don't forget the apple sauce! Serves 8-10.

★*Peggy McAlpine*

SWEET AND PUNGENT PORK

Perfect for a special dinner.

2	tablespoons salad oil	1	can (10 ounces) pineapple
2	cups sliced celery		chunks
1	green pepper, cut into	1/4	cup sugar
	strips	1	clove garlic, minced
1	pound lean pork, cut	1	teaspoon salt
	into 1/2-inch cubes	2	teaspoons soya sauce
2	tablespoons corn starch	1/3	cup vinegar
1	cup consommé		hot cooked rice

In a medium-sized saucepan, heat oil, salt and garlic. Brown pork in it. Add 1/3 of the consommé and the pineapple, simmer covered 1/2 hour. Add green pepper and celery. Cook 10 to 15 minutes more. Blend remaining ingredients, stir into meat, cook until thickened. Serves 6.

★*Linda Dyer*

SHERRY PORK TENDERLOIN

This pork tenderloin tastes almost better cold. With a vegetable salad, hot bread, and some interesting mustard — a memorable summer lunch.

1/2 cup soy sauce	4	garlic cloves, minced
1/2 cup dry sherry	1	pork tenderloin (about 1 1/2
1/4 cup peeled and minced		pounds)
gingerroot		

In a glass bowl combine soy sauce, sherry, gingerroot and garlic. Prick tenderloin all over with a fork, add it to marinade and let it marinate, covered and refrigerated, overnight. Drain, reserving marinade. Broil the tenderloin, basting occasionally with some of the marinade, for 20 minutes (turning it once). Let it stand for 10 minutes. Slice, and pour leftover marinade (which has been heated) over. Serves 4.

★*Valda Ondaatje*

SWEET AND SOUR SPARERIBS

Fry 2 pounds spareribs until brown all over. Place in large casserole or roaster. Add enough flour to the fat in the frying pan to absorb all the fat. Add 6 cups water and stir until thickened. Add:

$1/_3$ cup brown sugar	2 cups chopped celery
$1/_2$ cup vinegar	$1/_4$ cup each of green pepper
$1/_2$ cup ketchup	and sweet red pepper,
2 large onions, chopped	chopped

Pour all ingredients over spareribs. Place casserole in a 350°F. oven. Bake for $1^1/_2$ hours, stirring occasionally. Serves 4.

★*Olive G. Dorey*

SAUSAGE SUPPER

Simple but very tasty — good on a cold night.

1¹/₂ pounds sausage meat
1 green pepper, chopped
2 green onions
2 or 3 celery stalks, chopped

2 cups chicken consommé or boullion
1 cup raw rice
1 tablespoon Worcestershire sauce
¹/₂ teaspoon salt

Crumble sausage in a skillet and brown. Pour off a little fat. Then add the other ingredients. Simmer at low heat for 1 hour. Serves 6.

★*Linda Dyer*

SPARERIBS WITH APPLES AND SAUERKRAUT

Sauerkraut in Nova Scotia was a staple winter vegetable in the days before refrigeration. Here is a recipe which makes a hearty winter stew.

3¹/₂ to 4 pounds meaty spareribs
1 tablespoon butter or oil
1 quart fresh sauerkraut, washed under cold water, squeezed dry
1 medium carrot, grated
2 teaspoons caraway seeds

³/₄ teaspoon salt
¹/₄ teaspoon pepper
2 medium onions, thinly sliced
3 large tart apples, cored and cut into rings
1¹/₂ cups dry white wine or chicken stock

Pre-heat oven to 350°F. Cut the spareribs into serving portions. Quickly brown them in butter or oil in large skillet. Combine sauerkraut, carrot, caraway seeds, salt and pepper. Place half of the mixture in a buttered roasting pan. Cover with half the onions and apples. Top with browned spareribs. Cover with remaining sauerkraut mixture; top with remaining onions and apples. Pour wine over all. Bake, covered, for 1¹/₂ hours. Serves 4.

★Mrs. Harry Hutt

GRANNY'S SWEET AND SOUR BEEF SHORT RIBS

This is my grandmother's recipe for sweet and sour beef short ribs. It is for approximately six pounds of ribs, but can be adjusted for more or less.

6	tablespoons cornstarch	1¹/₂	teaspoons salt
³/₄	cup vinegar (white)	9	tablespoons soya sauce
³/₄	cup white sugar	3	cups *cold* water
		6	pounds beef ribs

Combine vinegar, sugar, water, soya sauce and salt. Heat mixture until it boils. Mix cornstarch with small amount of water (saved from 3 cups) and when the mixture boils, pour the cornstarch in. To cook the meat, cut ribs into small serving pieces. Place these in a pot which has a small amount of oil in the bottom. Cook, over slow heat, for 2 to 3 hours. When meat is tender, drain off all fat and then add soya sauce mixture. Let entire mixture simmer slowly for another hour.

Serve over hot rice or egg noodles with a tossed salad. Serves 6-8.

★Gail Walker

There was once a young woman from Chester
Who entered a gourmet fiesta
Her cheese-dip was fun
But her tarts soaked in rum
Were definitely the pièce-de-resista'!

BEEF WELLINGTON

Perfect for a very special dinner.

Pastry Ingredients

5   cups sifted flour
1   teaspoon salt
4   ounces butter, cut into
    $^1/_2$-ounce pieces
    and chilled

4   ounces shortening cut into
    $^1/_2$-ounce pieces, chilled
1   egg, lightly beaten
4   ounces iced water

Filling Ingredients

1   fillet of beef — about
    3-3$^1/_2$ pounds,
    fat removed
1   teaspoon brandy
$^1/_2$ teaspoon salt

$^1/_4$ teaspoon black pepper
6   slices bacon
8   ounces pâté de foie gras or
    chicken liver pâté
1   egg, lightly beaten

Sauce Ingredients

3   ounces butter
6   shallots, finely chopped

2$^1/_2$ cups beef stock
5   ounces plus one tablespoon
    Madeira

Preheat oven to 450°F. Sift flour into medium-sized bowl. Add salt, butter and shortening and rub butter and shortening into flour until it resembles fine bread crumbs. With a wooden spoon stir in beaten egg and enough ice water to make firm dough. Using hands, pat, and lightly knead dough. Wrap in waxed paper and chill for 30 minutes. Rub fillet with brandy and sprinkle with salt and pepper. Cover top of meat with bacon slices. Place meat on rack in roaster and bake 15 to 20 minutes for rare — 5 minutes longer, for medium. Remove from oven, remove bacon, let cool. When room temperature, spread pâté over top and sides of meat. Reduce oven temperature to 375°F., enclose meat in pastry, and bake until pastry is brown and crisp. Serves 6-8.

★*Terry Kierans*

SHIRLEY'S LASAGNA

This recipe makes a large lasagna, serving 12 to 16, with a small one for the freezer. It is very moist, running with cheese, and very good.

Meat Sauce

1	large can tomatoes	2	pounds hamburger
1	small can tomato paste	2	pounds onions
$1/_2$	pound mushrooms, sliced	2	cloves garlic
	basil and oregano, to taste		

Fry hamburger, onions and garlic. Drain the oil and, in a saucepan, combine hamburger mixture with rest of ingredients and simmer for $1^1/_2$ hours.

Lasagna

4	cups cottage cheese	2	pounds lasagna noodles,
2	eggs		cooked
1	pound mozzarella		Romano cheese
	cheese, grated		

Spread meat sauce on the bottom of a large, rectangular, ovenproof dish; arrange a layer of noodles on top, add another layer of sauce, then a layer of cottage cheese and sprinkle mozzarella and Romano over top. Repeat with another layer. Bake in a 350°F. oven for 30 to 45 minutes until browned and bubbling. Serves 12-16.

★*Shirley Moody*

BEEF BOURGUIGNON

A wonderful party dish — it tastes even better if made the day before.

2 **pounds chuck, or top round of beef**	$1/2$ **teaspoon instant minced garlic**
$1/4$ **cup flour**	$1/4$ **cup fresh parsley**
$1/4$ **cup butter**	3 **cups carrots, chopped in circles**
1 **bay leaf**	2 **cups beef broth**
$1^1/_2$ **teaspoons salt, or to taste**	1 **cup wine (red burgundy)**
$3/4$ **teaspoon thyme leaves**	12 **small onions**
3 **cups fresh mushrooms, sliced**	$1/2$ **teaspoon freshly ground pepper**
	1 **tablespoon butter**

Trim off and discard excess fat from meat. Cut meat into 1-inch cubes. Roll in flour. Melt butter in heavy quart saucepan; add meat, stir and cook until browned (a few at a time). Stir in all remaining flour; cook 1 minute; add salt, bay leaf, garlic, parsley, carrots, beef broth and wine. Cover and simmer for $1^3/_4$ hours, or until meat is almost tender. Meanwhile, peel onions and add. Cover, and cook for 30 minutes; add thyme and pepper. Sauté mushrooms in 1 tablespoon of butter and add. Cover and cook 5 minutes, add $1/4$ cup of wine 2 minutes before removing from heat. Serve hot over potatoes, rice or noodles. Serves 6.

★*Betty McInnes*

MEAT LOAF

The applesauce makes the difference.

1 **pound hamburger**	$1/4$ **cup onion, minced**
$1/2$ **cup thick, unsweetened**	$1^1/4$ **teaspoons salt**
applesauce	$1/8$ **teaspoon pepper**
1 **egg, well-beaten**	$1/4$ **cup ketchup**
$1/2$ **cup soft bread crumbs,**	
packed	

Mix the first 7 ingredients together and put into a loaf pan. Pour over ketchup, mixed with an equal amount of water. Bake at 350°F. for $1^1/4$ hours. Serves 4.

★*Betty L. Bezanson*

DINNER IN A DISH

This is a very easy supper dish.

4 **tablespoons butter**	$1/4$ **teaspoon pepper**
1 **medium onion, chopped**	2 **eggs, beaten**
2 **green peppers, chopped**	2 **cups cream style corn**
1 **pound hamburger**	4 **medium tomatoes, sliced**
1 **teaspoon salt**	$1/2$ **cup dry bread crumbs**

Sauté onion and green peppers in butter for 3 minutes. Add meat and blend together with seasoning. Remove from heat. Stir in eggs and mix well. Put 1 cup corn in buttered baking dish, then half the meat mixture, then a layer of sliced tomatoes. Repeat layers and top with buttered bread crumbs. Bake at 375°F. for 35 minutes. Serves 4-6.

★*Margaret Corkum*

VEGETABLE MEAT LOAF

With hot rolls and a salad, a very satisfying meal.

1¹/₂ pounds ground beef	¹/₂ teaspoon salt
1 medium onion, finely chopped	¹/₄ teaspoon pepper
¹/₂ cup chopped green pepper	¹/₂ teaspoon dry mustard
¹/₂ cup chopped celery	¹/₈ teaspoon cayenne pepper
2 cups carrots, shredded or grated	¹/₂ teaspoon Worcestershire sauce
1 cup bread crumbs	1 tin tomato soup, undiluted
1 egg, lightly beaten	

Combine all ingredients, blending thoroughly. Press into greased loaf pan. Bake 350°F. for 1¹/₂ hours. Serves 6.

★Marion Mulrooney

AMERICAN CHOP SUEY

Always a family favourite.

1 pound hamburger	1 cup milk
2 cups macaroni	3 tablespoons cheese
1 can tomato soup	2 medium onions, chopped
	salt and pepper

Cook hamburger in frying pan with the onion; add salt and pepper, to taste. Boil macaroni in salted water until tender. Mix meat and macaroni in casserole. Add tomato soup, milk and cheese. Bake for 45 minutes to an hour in a slow (325°F.) oven. More cheese or seasoning may be added if desired. Serves 4.

★Betty L. Bezanson

QUICKEST, EASIEST, TASTIEST CHESTER BEEF STEW

The secret ingredient is the minute tapioca. One can also add carrots, turnips, potatoes, etc. during the first hour of cooking. Believe it or not it's delicious!

$3^1/_2$ pounds cubed beef	2 tins consommé
2 medium onions, chopped	$2^1/_2$ cups hot water
5 tablespoons minute tapioca	2 4-ounce cans sliced mushrooms
salt and pepper, to taste	

Combine and mix all ingredients in casserole dish; cover and bake for 4 hours at 300°F. Serve with rice or use a pastry topping. Serves 8.

★ *Janet Piers*

SPAGHETTI AND MEAT CASSEROLE

A pasta dish that can be prepared ahead of time and baked just before serving.

5 ounces spaghetti, cooked according to package directions	$3/_4$ pound ground beef
	$1^1/_2$ cups tomato juice
1 tablespoon oil	$1/_2$ cup ketchup
$1/_4$ cup chopped onion	2 teaspoons Worcestershire sauce
$1^1/_2$ teaspoons salt	Parmesan cheese

Brown onions in oil. Add $1/_2$ teaspoon salt and ground beef and brown slightly. Mix tomato juice, ketchup, Worcestershire sauce, and 1 teaspoon salt. Combine meat and spaghetti in greased casserole and top with sauce. Bake in a 375°F. oven for 30 minutes. Serve sprinkled with Parmesan. Serves 4.

★*Leith Zinck*

SCRUMPTIOUS SPAGHETTI SAUCE

Don't pucker too much — and have fun slurping!

4 or 5 cloves garlic, minced
1¹/₂ or 2 onions, finely chopped
5 tablespoons olive oil
2 large cans Italian tomatoes
1 large can tomato paste
1 bay leaf
1 teaspoon Italian seasoning
6 peppercorns
4 or 5 cloves,
whole mushrooms, fresh or canned, if desired

1 small green pepper, minced
¹/₂ red pepper, minced
¹/₂ teaspoon (or more to taste) oregano
¹/₄ cup finely chopped fresh parsley
2 carrots, finely grated
1¹/₂ teaspoons salt (more, to taste, if necessary)
¹/₂ teaspoon basil (or less)
¹/₄ cup sugar, dissolved in scant cup of boiling water

Brown garlic, onions and peppers in a heavy pot with olive oil. Add tomatoes, tomato paste, bay leaf, seasoning, peppercorns, cloves, oregano, parsley, carrots, salt, basil, mushrooms and sugar. Cover and simmer over low heat for 2 hours. Uncover and simmer until serving time (another couple of hours).

★*Bertie Baker*

Meat **97**

VEAL ROLLS

Round steak may be substituted for the veal.

2 pounds veal cutlets, $^1/_4$ inch thick	2 tablespoons oil
2 cups soft bread crumbs	1 can consommé
1 tablespoon chopped parsley	$^1/_4$ cup dry red or white wine
2 tablespoons chopped onion	1 clove garlic
$^1/_4$ cup butter	1 teaspoon paprika
$^1/_4$ cup finely chopped mushrooms	$^1/_4$ cup flour
$^1/_4$ cup stuffed olives	dash of pepper
	1 teaspoon salt

Cut cutlets into 6 serving pieces. Place between two sheets of wax paper and pound until thin. Heat butter in a heavy skillet and cook onion, parsley and mushrooms in it until limp. Combine with crumbs and chives, salt and pepper. Divide stuffing evenly among the veal; roll up tightly, tying with string. Combine flour and paprika and coat rolls. Heat cooking oil in a heavy skillet; add rolls and brown well. Place in a shallow baking dish which has been rubbed with the garlic. Drain off oil in skillet. Add $^1/_4$ cup red or white wine and the consommé and scrape up all the brown bits. Pour over the veal rolls and bake in a 350°F. oven, covered, for about one hour or until tender, turning the rolls once. Serve with hot buttered noodles, or, rice if you prefer. You may like to thicken the sauce with a teaspoon of flour in some red wine. Serves 6.

★*Joan Rounsfell*

For exotic flavour
In your chowder
Add a taste
Of curry powder.

REALLY EXCEPTIONAL LAMB STEW

The flavour will be richer if the stew (but not the vegetables) is prepared several days ahead and then refrigerated to mellow.

The Broth

2   pounds or more lamb bones and 1 pound piece of neck
2   leeks
2   large onions
2   large carrots
1   turnip
1   teaspoon rosemary
2 or 3 sprigs parsley
3   garlic cloves, crushed
    salt
2 to 3 quarts water

The Stew

4   pounds lamb shoulder, cut into 1$^1/_2$ inch cubes
    flour
5   tablespoons butter
2   garlic cloves, minced
12 small carrots
3   small turnips, peeled and quartered
3   leeks, cut into 2-inch pieces
1   pound green beans
3 to 4 tablespoons butter, kneaded with the same amount of flour
    chopped parsley

It is best to start the dish a day in advance. Make the broth first. Brown the bones and neck in a hot 425° to 450°F. oven. Combine them with the vegetables, seasonings and water. Simmer 4 to 5 hours. Cool overnight. Then skim off the fat, strain the broth and set aside.

Dredge the meat with flour and brown in the butter. Transfer to a large Dutch oven or braising pot. Add enough boiling lamb broth to just cover the meat, and return to a boil. (Or use $^2/_3$ broth, $^1/_3$ white wine.) Rinse the pan used for browning with a little more of the broth and add to the meat. Simmer covered for one hour or until the meat is just tender. Drain, and reserve the broth. Keep the meat warm. In the meantime cook the vegetables in boiling salted water — the carrots and turnips in one pot, the onions and leeks in another, and the green beans in a third.

Add some of the vegetable juices to the meat broth, and reduce over a rather brisk heat. If you like, thicken the sauce slightly with butter and flour kneaded together, and stir until smooth. Taste for seasoning. Combine with the meat, carrots, turnips, onions and leeks, and just heat through. Add the green beans and heat another moment. Serve on a hot platter, surrounded with mounds of steamed rice, and garnish with chopped parsley. Serves 8-10.

★*Valda Ondaatje*

HAMBURGER MACARONI CASSEROLE

Experiment with the seasonings. Basil or chili peppers are good additions.

2 tablespoons oil	2 teaspoons salt
$1/_2$ cup chopped onion	$1/_4$ teaspoon celery salt
1 pound ground beef	$1/_8$ teaspoon pepper
$3^1/_2$ cups canned tomatoes	1 teaspoon Worcestershire
1 cup diced celery	sauce
chopped parsley	1 8-ounce package elbow
$1^1/_2$ cups chopped green	macaroni
pepper	grated cheese
1 cup sliced mushrooms	

Cook macaroni and drain. Melt fat and sauté onions, mushrooms, celery and green pepper. Remove from pan and brown the ground beef. Add to the meat tomatoes, sautéed vegetables, seasoning and cooked macaroni. Bring to a boil and lower heat and simmer for 35 - 45 minutes. Sprinkle parsley and cheese on each serving. Serves 4.

★*Hilda Tzagarakis*

Vegetables

Chester Train Station

BUTCH'S DANDELION GREENS

The first spring dandelions are the most tender, but even late summer dandelions make a tasty dish — when done this way.

1 pound dandelion leaves	$^1/_4$ pound bacon, chopped
4 tablespoons cider vinegar	2 tablespoons butter
	salt, to taste

Wash greens in several changes of cold water until all grit is removed. Put into saucepan with a little water, and steam. When boiling, add 1 tablespoon vinegar. Let boil until tender (5 to 8 minutes). Add 2 or more tablespoons of vinegar.

Meanwhile, fry bacon until crisp. Drain dandelion greens, add another tablespoon of vinegar and two of butter. Combine with bacon bits and some of the bacon fat; stir and serve. Serves 4.

★*Butch Heisler*

A CHESTER RATATOUILLE

This recipe evolved from reading several authentic ones last summer. It was made with the fruits of our Chester garden, and there are still several jars left to enjoy while this year's garden is growing.

1¹/₂ cups chopped onions
2¹/₂ pounds tomatoes—
about 4¹/₂ cups, peeled and chopped
³/₄ cup fresh basil leaves— tightly packed and chopped coarsely
3 smallish zucchini, cut up, not peeled

2 to 3 small eggplants, cut up
¹/₂ green pepper
1 red pepper
1 cup tomato purée (canned)
2 or 3 garlic cloves, minced
olive oil
salt and pepper, to taste

Chop onions and sweat them in a covered heavy pan with a spoonful of olive oil, until transparent. Remove seeds and stems from peppers and cut them into thin strips. Sauté them in a spoonful of olive oil. Sauté the garlic in oil and add the herbs, tomatoes and tomato paste. Cook, stirring to make a thick purée—you will need more olive oil. Cook zucchini and eggplant, simmering with a little oil — when cooked so that pieces pierce easily with a fork, continue in a large pot. Add tomatoes and herb mixture, and continue to stir until vegetables are well mixed with tomatoes. Take off heat, and if too much oil on top, spoon it off. Serves a crowd!

★*Marian Straus*

CORN ON A PICNIC

There is no better way of cooking very fresh corn.

corn on the cob

Leave husks and silk on corn. Take each ear and dip in heavily salted water. Cook in hot ashes, turning frequently so that it will be evenly cooked on all sides. If you have a pair of asbestos gloves in your outdoor cooking equipment, wear these, and turn the corn by hand.

★*Marian Straus*

CORN RING

Serve mushroom sauce with this for a luncheon dish — or, instead, with mushrooms and other seasonal vegetables.

2	pint-cans corn (cream style, yellow)	white pepper
2	scant cups cream	cayenne
8	eggs, separated	paprika
2	teaspoons salt	

To corn, add well-beaten egg yolks, salt, white pepper, cayenne and paprika to taste. Add cream and then stiffly beaten egg whites. Put in a well buttered ring mould, set in a bain marie and bake in a moderate oven for $1/2$ hour, or until set. Remove to hot platter — fill centre with sautéed mushrooms.

Mushroom Sauce

Peel mushrooms, remove stems and slice fairly thin. Take one good tablespoon sweet butter and simmer the mushrooms slowly for 5 minutes. Strain. Take one heaping tablespoon of flour, let cook in the butter but do not brown. Add 1 cup chicken broth and 2 tablespoons cream, then add mushrooms and heat thoroughly.

★*Marian Straus*

CORN SCALLOP

Good with cold cuts and a salad.

2 cups canned corn	1 tablespoon flour
1 cup milk	salt and pepper
1¹/₂ cups cracker crumbs	piece of butter
1 egg	

Mix flour in milk and add to corn. Add beaten egg and cracker crumbs, salt and pepper. Put in baking dish and sprinkle with crumbs and dot of butter. Bake in a fairly hot oven, about ¹/₂ hour. Serves 4.

★*Leta Udall*

RAW POTATO HASH

A traditional Tancook Island dish.

small piece salt pork	1 teaspoon summer savory
3 medium potatoes	water
1 onion	

Cut the piece of pork into cubes and fry until browned. Slice potatoes and onion, add savory and add all to brown pork. Cover halfway with water. Simmer, covered, for 20 to 25 minutes. Turn potatoes every 5 minutes or so. Serves 2.

★*G. Nunn*

INDIAN VEGETABLE CURRY

Excellent with chicken and rice.

1 small head cauliflower, cut into florets	2 teaspoons ground cumin
2 medium potatoes, cut into pieces	1 teaspoon turmeric
1/2 cup oil	1 teaspoon red pepper (cayenne, or flakes of freshly cut up)
	fresh or frozen peas (optional)

Heat oil in a skillet and add spices. Cook a bit, then add vegetables and 3 cups water. If desired add peas. Cook until tender. Serves 6.

★*Eleanor Seyffert*

MAY ROSE'S "HOT POTATOES"

Easy, delicious — and very hot potatoes!

potatoes	hot Mexican chili pepper flakes
butter	lemon pepper (optional)

Boil potatoes in their skins until tender. Cool and peel. Cut them to desired size. Melt some butter in a pot. Add the potatoes.

Sprinkle amply with hot Mexican chili pepper flakes. Stir and cook for a little while and serve immediately. May be sprinkled with some lemon pepper for additional piquancy.

★*Eleanor Seyffert*

POTATO SKINS

These are really crunchy and delicious.

potatoes
butter

pepper
Tabasco
garlic salt

Bake potatoes and remove all the insides. Using scissors, cut the skins in strips about one inch wide. Put on a baking sheet; brush generously with melted butter; season with garlic salt, freshly ground black pepper, and a little Tabasco. Put in a 475°F. oven or under the broiler until they are brown and crisp. Serve as an appetizer or as a vegetable.

★*Janet Ondaatje*

GERMAN KOL SLAW

Delicious with fried, well-drained pork scraps or bacon.

1   head cabbage, cut-up
$^1/_2$ cup brown sugar

$^1/_2$ cup margarine
salt and pepper, to taste

Combine all ingredients and cook slowly on top of stove for $^3/_4$ to one hour. Best if stored overnight, but serve hot.

★*Elizabeth Pellow*

DRESSED SWISS CHARD

Best when picked from your own garden.

swiss chard
olive oil

lemon juice
salt

Cut stalks into 2-inch pieces and cook in a big pot of salted water. Cut up the leaves and add to the pot. Cook for 5 minutes — do not overcook. Drain well. Put in serving dish and add 2 parts olive oil to 1 part lemon juice, enough to coat leaves and stalks well. Season with salt, to taste, and serve.

★*Eleanor Seyffert*

BAKED SQUASH AND RICE

Goes wonderfully well with chicken.

1$^1/_2$ pounds yellow squash
3 cups cooked rice
$^1/_2$ cup chopped green
   pepper
$^1/_2$ cup chopped onion
$^1/_2$ cup mayonnaise

$^1/_2$ cup milk
1 can chicken soup
2 eggs, beaten
1 teaspoon salt
   pepper
1 cup grated cheddar cheese

Slice squash and boil for 5 minutes and drain. In a large bowl, mix rice, squash, green pepper and onion. In another bowl beat eggs and add mayonnaise, milk and soup, salt and pepper. Mix thoroughly and add to rice mixture. Pour into greased, shallow 2-quart casserole. Cover with grated cheese. Bake at 350°F. for 30 minutes. Serves 8.

★*Clarissa Gibbs*

SQUASH CASSEROLE

An excellent dish for a buffet dinner. Can be made ahead of time
and kept warm.

2 pounds squash (2 cups)	1 cup sour cream
$^1/_4$ cup onion, minced	1 8-ounce package herb
1 can cream of chicken	stuffing
soup	$^1/_2$ cup butter

Sauté squash and onion. Drain. Combine soup and sour cream.
Fold in cooked squash. Line the bottom of a casserole with half of
herb stuffing, pour in vegetables and top with the rest of stuffing.
Bake in a 350°F. oven for 25 to 30 minutes. Serves 6.

★*Marjorie Capon*

BAKED ZUCCHINI OR YELLOW SUMMER SQUASH

A very useful recipe — a vegetable dish that will wait for the
meat.

2 pounds zucchini or	basil
squash	ketchup
3 medium onions	salt and pepper
Hygrade bacon bits	

Slice zucchini or squash. Slice onions and separate into rings.
Cook rings in oil for 5 minutes. In a casserole, make layers of
zucchini, salt, pepper, a little basil, ketchup dots, then onions and
bacon bits. Repeat. Cover and bake at 350°F. for 1 hour. Serves 4.

★*Dee Dee Blain*

RICE TREAT

Especially good with chicken or fish.

3 cups Minute rice	2 chicken bouillon cubes, dissolved in 1 cup boiling water
2 cups chicken broth from soup stock	
1 teaspoon, plus, fines herbes	4 or 5 fresh chives, chopped

Bring stock and all other ingredients to rolling boil. Add rice; cover. Turn off heat. Allow to stand 5 minutes. Serve. Serves 4-6.

★*Bertie Baker*

RICE ROYALE

A very tasty way of cooking rice.

2 cups Minute rice	2 soup cans water
8 tablespoons olive oil	2 tablespoons soy sauce
2 cans consommé mushrooms, if desired — about $1/_2$ pound	4 green onions, finely chopped

Mix all ingredients and bake in a buttered casserole at 350°F. for $1^1/_4$ hours, or until done.

★*Bertie Baker*

ZUCCHINI DINNER

Really a vegetable stew — wonderful with beef.

6   zucchini, seeded and cut into 2-inch pieces
2   onions, chopped
4   potatoes, diced
2   cups celery leaves
2   stalks celery, diced
1   medium can seasoned tomatoes
3   tablespoons olive oil
    salt and pepper to taste
4   basil leaves or 1 teaspoon crushed basil

Place fresh vegetables in pan or Dutch oven. Cover with the remaining ingredients. Cover and simmer gently for 1 hour, stirring occasionally. Serves 6.

★Una Redden

MACARONI-CHEDDAR SALAD

Wonderful with rare roast beef.

3   cups macaroni
1   cup sour cream
1   cup mayonnaise
$1/_4$ cup milk
$1/_2$ cup sweet relish
2   tablespoons vinegar
2   teaspoons prepared mustard
$3/_4$ teaspoon salt
2   cups Cheddar cheese, cubed
1   cup celery, chopped
$1/_2$ cup green pepper, chopped
$1/_4$ cup onion, chopped

Cook macaroni until done. Drain, and set aside to cool. Combine sour cream, mayonnaise, milk, relish, vinegar, mustard and salt in a bowl. Toss together cold macaroni, cheese, celery, green pepper, and onion. Pour sour cream mixture over all and toss lightly to mix. Chill several hours or overnight.

★Elaine Heisler

CHESTER SAUERKRAUT SALAD

If you use fresh sauerkraut, cook first for about 3 hours.

1 large can sauerkraut
   (28 ounces)
1 small bottle chopped
   pimento
1 cup celery, grated or
   chopped
$^1/_2$ cup oil

1 medium onion, grated or
   chopped (you can use green
   pepper)
1 level cup cider vinegar
$1^3/_4$ (or less) cup sugar

Drain and squeeze sauerkraut well. Add pimento, celery, onion or green pepper and pour oil over all. Boil vinegar and sugar together for 5 minutes and pour over sauerkraut. Let stand in refrigerator for 3 days before serving. Serves 6.

★*Ruth Gibson*

CABBAGE, PINEAPPLE AND MARSHMALLOW SALAD

An unusual blend of flavours; good as a winter salad when fresh greens are sometimes hard to find.

3 cups cabbage, shredded
$^3/_4$ cup drained crushed
   pineapple
$^1/_4$ cup cream
$^1/_2$ cup mayonnaise

salt and pepper
few grains cayenne
1 cup marshmallows, cut into
   pieces

Mix pineapple and cabbage together. Add cream to mayonnaise and mix well. Add seasoning. Mix dressing with cabbage and pineapple; add marshmallow. Toss lightly. Keep cool. Serves 6.

★*Marjorie Capon*

SAUERKRAUT SALAD

A traditional Nova Scotian specialty.

$^2/_3$ cup white vinegar
$^1/_3$ cup water
$^1/_2$ cup oil
1 cup sugar

3 cups sauerkraut
1 green pepper, chopped
1 cup celery, diced
1 large onion, sliced into rings

Blend first four ingredients and add sauerkraut, then rest of ingredients. Refrigerate overnight. Serves 6.

★Mrs. Dale Barkhouse

The best of cooking
Finest tastes
Are lost if you don't
Warm your plates.

BIG HILL DRESSING

Delicious with lettuce fresh out of the garden.

12 ounces salad oil
4 ounces white vinegar
10 ounce tin of tomato soup
2 tablespoons white sugar
1 teaspoon dry mustard

1 teaspoon salt
dash of pepper
dash of Worcestershire
sauce
1 small onion, cut up
1 small green pepper, cut up

Whirl all together in a blender and store in covered jar in refrigerator.

★H.F. Pullen

WARWICK HOTEL LA MAIS SAUCE

Good with cold meat.

1 pint mayonnaise	1 tablespoon celery, finely chopped
$^1/_2$ bottle chili sauce	
$^1/_4$ cup India relish	1 slice pimento
1 tablespoon Worcestershire sauce	$^1/_2$ teaspoon dry mustard
	$^1/_2$ teaspoon black pepper
2 hard-boiled eggs, finely chopped	$^1/_2$ teaspoon paprika
	$^1/_2$ teaspoon sugar
$^1/_4$ green pepper	

Mix all ingredients together in a large bowl (make sure it is really well mixed). Chill in refrigerator. Makes 1 quart.

★*Alberta Pew*

PENNSYLVANIA RAILROAD
SALAD DRESSING

Try this over sliced beefsteak tomatoes.

1   can Campbell's Tomato
    Soup
1   cup vinegar
1   cup sugar
1   cup Wesson or Mazola oil
1   teaspoon salt

1   teaspoon dry mustard
    pinch pepper or paprika
1   small onion, grated
1   clove garlic

Mix and put in refrigerator for 2 hours before using. Makes 1 quart.

★*Alberta Pew*

CELERY SEED DRESSING

A sweet but tangy dressing.

1   cup salad oil
1/2 cup sugar (scant)
1/3 cup ketchup
1/3 cup vinegar

1   teaspoon celery seed
1   teaspoon paprika
1   teaspoon salt
1   tablespoon grated onion

Combine all ingredients and shake well. Store in refrigerator. If you prefer a creamy dressing, place all ingredients in a blender except oil. Blend, and slowly add the oil.

★*Joan Rounsfell*

Luncheon Dishes

SUNDAY MORNING BREAKFAST
IN CHESTER

This Sunday breakfast was my contribution to a family celebration held over a long weekend in Chester last summer. I planned to do it on the beach at 10 a.m., and, as people gathered, bull shots were hot and waiting. With the aid of a hibachi and an open beach fire, we cooked the finnan haddie and the scrambled eggs and toasted the anadama bread. It was a memorable event.

Bull Shot

consommé **lemon slice**
vodka

Heat the consommé, add vodka and lemon.

Finnan Haddie

2 **onions** 1 **cup milk**
$^1/_2$ **pound smoked finnan** **coarse-ground pepper**
   haddie (per person), thick
   centre cut

In iron skillet, pour boiling water over finnan haddie. Drain. Then cover the fish with milk and add onion slices and grindings of coarse pepper. Simmer for 15 minutes. Serve hot.

Scrambled Eggs Cum Cottage Cheese

eggs (3 eggs for
two persons)
cottage cheese
garlic salt

pepper
tarragon

In Teflon pan, on medium heat, put 3 tablespoons of cottage cheese. Heat until it begins to liquify. Add eggs, which have been well beaten with wire whisk, and seasonings. Stir all ingredients constantly until cooked, but still moist.

Anadama Bread

2 cups boiling water
¹/₂ cup cornmeal
2 teaspoons salt
¹/₄ pound melted butter
(or Oleo)
¹/₄ cup wheat germ

¹/₂ cup molasses
¹/₂ cup warm water
1¹/₂ packages or cakes of yeast
4 cups flour, unbleached
handful of sesame seeds

Mix boiling water and cornmeal, and let it stand for one hour. Dissolve yeast in warm water. Add to cornmeal mixture together with remaining ingredients. Mix together. Let it stand, covered, in a warm place until it doubles in bulk. On a heavily floured board, knead dough several minutes and shape into two loaves. Cover and let rise in a warm place in bread pans until half an inch to top of pan. Bake in pre-heated oven at 350°F. for 40 minutes. Sprinkle sesame seeds on top of loaves before cooking.

★*Donald G. Grant*

POTATO ROMANOFF

A wonderful, simple lunch — good tasting, healthy, and different.

5 cups cooked, diced potatoes	1 cup sour cream
2 cups cottage cheese	$^1/_4$ cup minced onion
	bread crumbs
	grated cheese

Mix first four ingredients in a buttered casserole. Top with bread crumbs and grated cheese. Bake at 325°F. for 30 to 45 minutes. Serves 6.

★*Thirsty Thinkers Tea Room*

AVOCADOS STUFFED WITH
SCALLOPS AND RED CAVIAR

A beautiful presentation, but just as pleasing to the palate as to the eye.

$^1/_2$ cup dry white wine	juice of 1 lemon
$^1/_4$ cup scallops	salt and pepper, to taste
2 ripe avocados	4 tablespoons red caviar
$^1/_2$ cup sour cream	4 to 6 teaspoons finely chopped chives

Bring wine and $^1/_2$ cup water to a simmer, add scallops and cook over low heat for 2 to 3 minutes. Drain and refrigerate for 1 hour. Keep uncut avocados in refrigerator until the last moment.

Mix sour cream with 1 or 2 teaspoons of lemon juice and 2 or 3 grinds of pepper (do not add salt). Carefully stir in caviar, trying not to smash grains. Refrigerate.

When ready to serve, cut avocados in half lengthwise and discard pits. Sprinkle hollow of each avocado half with a bit of remaining lemon juice, a little salt (remember caviar is very salty!) and pepper, to taste. Fill hollows with scallops; top with caviar mixture. Serves 4.

★*Regis Dyer*

PHILIP BROWN'S ROMAINE SOUFFLÉ

You can make the base and fold in the egg whites an hour before baking, then leave in refrigerator until time to put in the oven.

1	large head of romaine	1	cup shredded Cheddar cheese
4	tablespoons butter	1	teaspoon salt
3	scallions, or green onion, chopped	$^1/_2$	teaspoon Worcestershire sauce
3	tablespoons flour		tabasco to taste
1	cup milk, heated		grated Parmesan cheese
4	eggs, separated		

Chop romaine (cleaned, drained). Put in heavy saucepan, with a little water, and cook until wilted. Drain and chop. Melt 1 tablespoon butter, cook scallions until soft, add romaine. Cook until moisture evaporates. Melt butter, blend flour, add milk. Cook until thick, then add yolks, cheese, and cook until smooth. Stir in romaine. Fold in whites. Bake in a soufflé dish (sprinkled in Parmesan) in preheated 400°F. oven, reduced to 375°F. and cook for 25 to 35 minutes. Serves 4.

★*Eleanor Seyffert*

CUCUMBER AND MINT SANDWICHES

Delicious with lemon tea!

wholewheat bread,
thinly sliced
cucumber
salt and pepper, to taste

mayonnaise
mint leaves

Butter one side of sandwich, spread mayonnaise on the other side. Place thinly sliced cucumber on the buttered side and rinsed and finely chopped fresh mint leaves on the mayonnaise side. Season with salt and pepper. Place together, remove crusts and slice into four triangles.

★H.F. Pullen

SCOTCH WOODCOCK

This is a very old family recipe and is copied exactly from my grandmother's recipe book.

Anchovy Butter
4 to 5 preserved anchovies
2   ounces unsalted butter

salt
pepper

Prepare anchovy butter by washing anchovies in warm water, then pounding them in a mortar with the butter. Keep in a cool place until required.

2 egg yolks	3 - 4 tablespoons whipping
1 ounce unsalted butter	cream
salt and pepper	1 teaspoon chopped parsley
	anchovy butter
	2 slices hot toast

Trim the slices of toast and spread with the anchovy butter. Pour over the hot sauce made as follows:

Put egg yolks, butter, cream, and parsley into a bowl, add seasoning. Stand the bowl over a pan of hot water and stir over the heat until the sauce thickens. Serve very hot. Serves 2.

★*Helen Dennis*

TORTILLAS DE MAIZ (CORN PANCAKES)

Delicious, served warm with sour cream and chopped parsley.

1 cup fresh corn kernels or	$1^1/_2$ teaspoons salt
defrosted frozen corn	$1/_2$ teaspoon freshly ground
$1/_3$ cup vegetable oil	black pepper
8 eggs	$1/_2$ cup sour cream
2 tablespoons flour	2 tablespoons finely chopped
	fresh parsley

Thoroughly dry kernels with paper towels. In a heavy 8 to 10 inch skillet, heat oil, drop in corn and cook, stirring for 10 minutes until corn is golden brown. Drain on paper towels.

In large bowl beat eggs, then beat in flour, salt and pepper. Melt 1 tablespoon butter in 5 to 6-inch skillet or crêpe pan set over moderate heat. Pour in $1/_4$ cup of batter. When edges begin to set, sprinkle the tortilla with 2 tablespoons of corn. With fork push the edges towards center to allow uncooked batter to run out.

When set, turn over with a spatula and cook 1 minute to brown the other side. Proceed similarly with remaining batter, adding a teaspoon of butter for each tortilla. Serve on individual plates with a tablespoon of sour cream and chopped parsley. Makes 8 (5 to 6-inch) pancakes.

★*Eleanor Seyffert*

BAKED BROWN BEANS WITH RUM

The rum and coffee make the difference!

3	**pounds dried pea beans**	2	**teaspoons salt**
$1/_2$	**pound salt pork, cut in small strips**	1	**cup chili sauce**
		$1/_2$	**cup strong coffee**
2	**onions, each stuck with a clove**	$1/_2$	**cup rum**
1	**cup molasses**		
$1^1/_2$	**teaspoons dry mustard**		

Soak beans overnight in cold water. Drain, and discard imperfect beans. Cover with fresh water and simmer over low heat until beans are tender but still whole (about 45 minutes). Drain beans, reserving the cooking water, and put them into a bean pot or deep baking dish with a cover. Bury the pork and the onions in the beans. Mix bean water with molasses, mustard, salt, and chili sauce and pour over the beans. Stir a little to mix, cover, and bake in a low oven (300°F.) for about 6 hours, adding water as needed so beans do not dry out. Pour the coffee and rum over the beans and cook them for 1 hour longer, uncovered. Serve in the baking dish. Serves 12-14.

★*Valda Ondaatje*

SAUSAGE PIE

Not difficult to make and a harmonious blend of flavours.

1 pound pork sausage meat	$^1/_2$ cup chopped onion
20 crackers, finely rolled or	10 ounces tomato soup
1 cup cracker crumbs	3 cups cooked rice
$^1/_2$ cup diced green pepper	1 cup grated Cheddar cheese

Brown sausage in skillet; drain off excess fat. Combine sausage, crackers, green pepper, onion and $^1/_2$ cup soup. Mix well and pat into shell in a deep 9-inch pie plate. Combine rest of soup with rice and cheese; pour into sausage crust. Bake at 350°F. for 35 to 40 minutes. Serves 6.

★*Linda Dyer*

CHEESE SOUFFLÉ

This recipe never fails.

6 slices white bread	2 cups milk
butter	1 teaspoon mustard (dry)
$^1/_2$ pound grated cheese	$^1/_2$ teaspoon salt
4 eggs	$^1/_2$ teaspoon pepper

Cut crusts off the bread and butter one side of slices. Cut into small cubes. In a buttered baking dish, put in a layer of bread and a layer of cheese. Repeat. Mix eggs, salt, milk, mustard, pepper, and beat them together. Pour over cheese and bread. Leave in refrigerator overnight and, prior to serving, bake 1 hour and 15 minutes at 375°F. Serves 4.

★*Jill Flinn*

BAKED BEANS DELUXE

This is a good Saturday night supper, served with brown bread.

2	pounds dried kidney beans	1	teaspoon dried sweet basil
1	28-ounce can Italian tomatoes	1	teaspoon dried mustard
		1	whole onion
1½-2	teaspoons salt, to taste	4	slices bacon, cut into quarters
1	cup molasses		

Soak beans overnight in water to cover by about 2 inches. Then simmer beans until tender. Drain, save water in which beans were cooked. Put cooked beans in buttered casserole with rest of ingredients. Stir well. Put bacon pieces on top. Add 1½ cups water in which beans were cooked. Cover. Bake for 3 to 6 hours at 300°F. Uncover for the last hour of cooking. If beans dry out during baking add some water. Serves 10 to 12.

★*Bertie Baker*

SMOKED FISH CASSEROLE

A traditional Nova Scotian specialty.

1	pound any smoked fish fillet	1½ to 2 cups milk	
3	tablespoons butter	cracker crumbs	
3	tablespoons flour		

Cover about 1 pound of any smoked fish in pan with cold water. Bring to a boil and pour water off. Repeat 3 times, then break fish into small pieces. Melt butter, add flour and stir until combined. Slowly add 1½ to 2 cups milk, stirring constantly until thickened. Add fish pieces. Pour into an ovenproof casserole. Cover with cracker crumbs and bake at 350°F. for 30 minutes. Serves 4.

★*Grace McClung*

A CRABMEAT LUNCHEON

Colourful and attractive, particularly when served in large scallop shells.

2 cups thin white sauce	**salt and pepper, to taste**
1 can crabmeat	**curry powder, to taste**
$1/_2$ jar pimento, finely chopped	**bread crumbs**
	grated cheddar cheese
$1/_4$ cup green pepper, finely chopped	
$1/_2$ cup celery, finely chopped	

Make a thin white sauce and place over a double boiler. Add crabmeat, finely chopped pimento, green pepper and celery. Season with salt, pepper, onion and a small amount of curry. Gently cook over hot water until flavours have melded.

Spoon into scallop shells. Cover with fine bread crumbs and grated cheddar cheese. Place under broiler until browned on top, and serve. Serves 4.

★*Helen Bethune*

EASY PIZZA

Children and adults alike love this pizza. The crust is made with baking powder, not yeast.

Dough Mix

6 **cups sifted flour**	$3/4$ **cup shortening**
4 **tablespoons baking powder**	
$1^1/2$ **teaspoons salt**	

Sift dry ingredients. Cut in shortening. This mixture can be stored in a covered jar in the refrigerator for up to 14 days. For each pizza, combine 2 cups mix and $3/4$ cup milk and mix together with a fork lightly. Turn out on a floured board and knead dough and crumbs together. Roll out to a 12-inch circle.

Filling

$1/2$ **cup chopped onion**	$1/2$ **teaspoon garlic salt**
$1/4$ **cup sliced mushrooms**	$1/2$ **teaspoon oregano**
$1/2$ **pound ground beef or** $1/4$	$1/2$ **teaspoon dill seed (optional)**
pound sliced pepperoni	$1/4$ **teaspoon pepper**
1 **6-ounce can tomato paste**	$1/2$ **pound mozzarella cheese,**
1 **8-ounce can tomato**	**grated**
sauce	**Parmesan cheese**

Mix all the ingredients except the Parmesan. Spread over the crust and brush with a little oil. Sprinkle with Parmesan. Bake in a 375°F. oven until crisp on top.

★*Hilda Tzagarakis*

A glass of Maritime good cheer
Is a single draught of Schooner beer.

BUMSTEADS

Children love these for lunch.

1 can white tuna or lobster
2 hard-boiled eggs, chopped
2 ounces cheddar cheese, chopped

1 onion, finely chopped
9 olives, finely chopped
9 pickles, finely chopped
  mayonnaise
4 hot dog rolls

Mix well and add mayonnaise to make a wet mixture. Fill hot dog rolls with the mixture. Heat rolls in 350°F. for about 20 minutes or until hot. Serves 4.

★*Nina Meisner*

ATOMIC SALAD

A variation of Niçoise.

2 cloves garlic
1 tablespoon wine vinegar (or cider vinegar)
  pinch of salt
  freshly ground pepper (20 turns)
  forkful of Dijon mustard
1/2 cup olive oil
  artichoke hearts

  avocado spears
  grated cheese
  lemon juice
  green onions
  sliced pepperoni
  sliced Spanish onions
  black olives
3 different kinds of lettuce

Press garlic in wooden salad bowl. Mix in vinegar, salt, pepper and mustard until frothy. Add oil. Add rest of ingredients and toss.

★*Eleanor Seyffert*

The sauerkraut question should be met head on. The fact is, lots of people do not like it, or think they don't. Most of the antipathy, however, is due to the fact that it requires careful grooming before being presented, and some cooks just don't take the trouble. Fresh sauerkraut tastes best, but any will be good if it's thoroughly rinsed to remove all but a hint of the pungent brine, and then braised in stock or wine.

4 slices bacon	$^1/_4$ cup brown sugar
1 small onion, chopped	2 cans (1 pound each) baked
1 pound sauerkraut, drained and washed	beans and pork
1 tart apple, chopped fine	2 tablespoons prepared mustard
$^1/_2$ cup stock or white wine	1 cup ketchup

Heat oven to 350°F. Fry bacon in skillet until crisp; drain on absorbent paper. Sauté onion in bacon drippings until soft. Combine sauerkraut, stock or white wine, apple, brown sugar, and onion with bacon drippings; mix well. Turn into 2-quart baking dish. Combine beans, mustard, and ketchup; spread over sauerkraut mixture. Bake, covered, 45 minutes. Remove cover. Place bacon strips on top of beans; bake 15 minutes longer. Serves 6.

★*Valda Ondaatje*

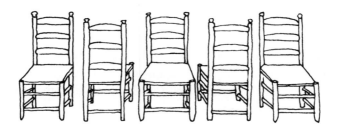

SPINACH SALAD

A useful main-course salad to have in one's repertoire.

Dressing

2	tablespoons white wine vinegar		salt
2	egg yolks		pepper
2	teaspoons Dijon mustard	2	cups oil
2	teaspoons chopped fresh tarragon or $^1/_2$ teaspoon dried		

2	pounds spinach, stemmed, washed and dried	$^1/_2$	pound bacon, crisply cooked, drained and chopped
3	cups shredded Swiss cheese	3	hard-boiled eggs, chopped
$^3/_4$	pound mushrooms, sliced		Tomato wedges (garnish)

Combine first 6 ingredients in medium bowl and blend well with whisk. Slowly add oil in steady stream, whisking constantly. Store in tightly covered container. (Can be refrigerated up to one week.)

Place spinach in large salad bowl. Add cheese, mushrooms, bacon, and eggs and toss with just enough dressing to coat lightly. Arrange on chilled individual plates and garnish with tomatoes. Serve with additional dressing. Serves 6.

★*Valda Ondaatje*

RICE AND CARROT BAKE

The mint gives this healthy casserole a very distinctive flavour.

2 cups brown rice, cooked	1 cup cottage cheese
1 cup carrots, ground	handful of parsley
1 teaspoon lemon juice	few sprigs of mint, chopped
1 can tuna or salmon	seasoning, to taste

Put all ingredients together in layers in a greased casserole. Bake in a 350°F. oven for 1 hour. Serves 4-6.

★*Mickie Haase*

CHICKEN STRATA

A wonderful dish for lunch — a very satisfying meal when served with a green salad.

8 slices day-old white bread	$3/_4$ teaspoon salt
2 cups chopped chicken or turkey	$1/_2$ teaspoon pepper
$1/_2$ cup chopped onion	$1/_2$ cup grated, sharp processed cheese
$1/_2$ cup chopped green pepper	2 slightly beaten eggs
$1/_2$ cup chopped celery	1 can cream of mushroom soup
$1/_2$ cup mayonnaise	

Butter 2 slices of bread; cut into $1/_2$ inch cubes. Set aside. Cut remaining bread into 1-inch cubes and place half of them in the bottom of an 8x8x2-inch casserole. Combine chicken, vegetables,

mayonnaise and seasonings and spoon over the bread cubes.
Sprinkle rest of cubes over the chicken mixture. Combine eggs
and milk. Pour over all the mixture. Chill for 1 hour or overnight.
Spoon soup over top and sprinkle with buttered bread cubes.
Bake at 325°F. for 50 minutes. Serves 6.

★*Hilda Tzagarakis*

SPINACH QUICHE

A rich, flavourful quiche — colourful and wholesome.

pastry for 9-inch pie	1 teaspoon horseradish
1 10-ounce package	4 tablespoons sour cream
frozen chopped spinach	$^1/_2$ cup grated Swiss cheese
$^1/_4$ teaspoon salt	4 tablespoons grated
freshly ground pepper	Parmesan cheese

Basic Custard

4 eggs	pinch of salt
$1^1/_2$ cups heavy cream	freshly ground pepper
$^1/_4$ cup dry white wine	pinch of nutmeg, freshly
	ground

Roll out and line a 9-inch tart pan or deep pie plate with pastry
and partially bake.

Cook the spinach until tender. Chop. Drain and dry thoroughly.
Add the salt and pepper, horseradish and sour cream. Spread the
mixture over the bottom of the pastry shell. Sprinkle with Swiss
and Parmesan cheeses. Cover with the custard and bake in
preheated 375°F. oven for 40 minutes or until custard is set and
golden brown. Cool slightly before serving. Serves 6.

★*Martha Woolley*

ALEX'S SOUR CREAM CLAM PIE

A very tempting blend of ingredients, and a welcome variation of the standard quiche.

2 cans (5 ounces each) baby clams	2 eggs, beaten
6 strips bacon, diced	1 cup sour cream
3/4 cup chopped onion	1/2 teaspoon salt
1/4 cup flour	paprika
dash pepper	1 unbaked 9-inch pie shell
2 drops Tabasco sauce	

Drain clams and reserve 3/4 cup liquor. Fry bacon until brown and add onion. Cook until tender. Blend in flour, then reserved liquor. Cook and stir until thick. Add clams, pepper, Tabasco. Stir a small amount into beaten eggs and return to mixture. Spoon into pie shell. Combine sour cream and salt, and spread over filling. Sprinkle with paprika.

Bake at 350°F. for 35 minutes until set. Let stand 10 minutes before serving. Good also as appetizer. Serves 4 as main course, 6-8 as appetizer.

★*Alex McCurdy*

DILLED NOVA SCOTIA CREPES

Make plain crêpe recipe — adding 3 tablespoons chopped dill — fresh from garden if possible. Crêpes may be frozen at this point if desired. Spread each crêpe half or quarter with sour cream or crème fraîche and top with a thin slice of smoked salmon. Sprinkle with pinch of dill. Fold in halves or quarters. Serve. Enjoy!

★*Beverley McInnes*

SCHOONER SALAD

It tastes as good as it looks!

1	pound fish fillets, cooked and flaked	1	fresh tomato, chopped
1	tablespoon lemon juice	$^1/_3$	cup mayonnaise
$^1/_2$	teaspoon salt	4	cucumbers, peeled and sliced in half lengthwise
1	cup chopped celery	8	lettuce leaves

Sprinkle fish with lemon juice and salt. Add celery and tomato and toss lightly with mayonnaise. Scoop out the pulp from cucumbers. Fill cucumber boats with mixture. Chill. Serve on lettuce leaves. Makes 8 boats.

★*Connie Stevens*

ALEX'S MAGIC SHELLFISH QUICHE

A quiche with a top, not a bottom.

$^1/_2$ pound Swiss cheese, grated

2 small cans lobster or crabmeat

3 tablespoons parsley, minced

1 large onion, chopped

4 large eggs

$1^1/_2$ cups milk or light cream

$^3/_4$ cup biscuit baking mix

salt, pepper

$^1/_4$ teaspoon nutmeg or mace

Preheat oven to 350°F. Mix cheese, lobster or crabmeat, parsley and onion and spread in bottom of greased deep quiche pan.

In blender, at high speed, mix eggs, milk, biscuit mix and spices. Pour over first mixture in pan and bake 50 minutes. Let stand for 10 minutes before serving. Good also as appetizer. Serves 4-6.

★ *Alex McCurdy*

STEAMED NUTMEAT

A meat loaf without meat.

4 shredded wheat biscuits

1 cup ground nuts (cashews, walnuts, almonds or pecans)

2 eggs

1 cup yogurt, approximately

handful of parsley

$^1/_2$ teaspoon sage or oregano

$^1/_4$ cup chopped onion (optional)

other seasonings to taste

Crumble shredded wheat. Combine with nuts, spices, eggs and enough yogurt to allow mixture to form a sticky ball. Press into greased quart steamer. Cover and steam over slowly boiling water for 2 hours — refilling water to within 1 inch of top of steamer when necessary (about 1 hour). Unmould while hot, and serve with a mushroom or tomato sauce, or, canned soup will do if time is a factor.

Variation — Put into loaf pan and bake in a 350°F. oven for 45 minutes. It may be sliced and served cold also.

★*Mickie Haase*

ROCKY CREST QUICHE

This quiche freezes very well.

1¹/₂ cups grated sharp cheese	¹/₂ teaspoon salt
1 tablespoon flour	dash cayenne pepper
¹/₂ pound bacon (fried and drained)	dash nutmeg
	¹/₂ cup milk
1 large onion	¹/₄ cup light cream
3 tablespoons butter	pastry shell
2 eggs	egg white

Mix cheese, flour and bacon together. Cut up large onion and sauté in butter. Beat eggs, salt, cayenne pepper and nutmeg in a large bowl. Add milk and cream. Line pastry shell in a pan with egg white (to coat) and bake in a 450°F. oven for 5 minutes. Remove from oven and cover with onion, bacon and cheese (preferably in that order). Pour egg mix on and bake at 450°F. for 30 minutes, and then at 350°F. for 10 minutes — inserted knife blade should come out clean. It is possible to freeze this quiche. Reheat at 250°F. for 20-30 minutes. May be used as hors d'ouevre or luncheon dish.

★*Alberta Pew*

SHRIMP CUSTARD CASSEROLE

Wonderful any time of year for lunch or as a light supper dish.

6 slices white bread (buttered and cubed)	2 cups milk
$^1/_2$ pound sharp Cheddar cheese, shredded	1 teaspoon salt
2 cans shrimp (5-ounce size)	$^1/_8$ teaspoon pepper
$^1/_4$ teaspoon dry mustard	$^1/_8$ teaspoon paprika
3 eggs, slightly beaten	few grains cayenne pepper

Arrange half the bread cubes in bottom of a greased 9-inch round or square baking dish. Sprinkle with half the cheese, shrimp and mustard. Make a second layer of remaining bread, shrimp and mustard; top with remaining cheese. Combine eggs, milk, salt, pepper, paprika, cayenne. Pour over bread and shrimp layers. Place baking dish in pan of hot water. Bake uncovered for 60 minutes in a 325°F. oven or until firm. Serves 4-6.

★*Connie Stevens*

MARDI GRAS CASSEROLE

A quick and easy dish to make when in a hurry. Also economical and tasty!

3 tablespoons flour
$^1/_4$ cup melted butter
$1^1/_2$ cups milk
$1^1/_2$ cups old cheese
$1^1/_2$ cups Minute rice
   chopped parsley
   cayenne

   paprika
$^1/_4$ teaspoon oregano
$1^1/_3$ cups water
1 pound can tomatoes
   onion
7 ounces solid tuna

Make cream sauce. Add cheese. Place Minute rice in pan, add herbs, $^2/_3$ cup drained tomatoes, onion, then tuna, cheese sauce and remaining tomatoes. Sprinkle with paprika. Bake approximately 15 minutes at 350°F. Serves 6.

★*Leith Zinck*

Breads

BROWN BREAD

Delicious with homemade strawberry jam.

5 cups lukewarm water	10 cups white flour
2 tablespoons yeast	$^3/_4$ cups wheat germ
$^1/_2$ cup honey	$^2/_3$ teaspoon salt
3 cups whole wheat flour	$^1/_4$ cup oil

Combine 5 cups lukewarm water with 2 tablespoons yeast; stir and let it foam. Add honey, whole wheat flour, 3 cups white flour, wheat germ. Beat 100 times, cover and let rise in a warm place for one hour. Fold in $^2/_3$ teaspoon salt, $^1/_4$ cup oil. Add remaining flour and knead until elastic. Oil bowl and top of bread. Let rise one hour covered, then punch down and let rise again (approximately 45 minutes, covered); punch down and cut into 4 pieces, knead gently into balls. Cover and leave on counter for 5 minutes. Oil pans. Shape loaves and put in pans. Let rise beside oven turned on to 350°F. Bake at 350°F. for 40 minutes. Yield: 4 loaves.

★*Kathleen Rowan-Legg*

BROWN SPOON BREAD

This is family recipe that was given to me as soon as I got married. Scottish in origin, it was handed down to each generation, and is still a stand-by in our house.

$^1/_2$ **cup cornmeal**	2$^1/_2$ **cups boiling water**
$^1/_2$ **cup rolled oats**	1 **cup molasses**
2 **teaspoons salt**	1 **tablespoon yeast**
$^1/_2$ **tablespoon butter**	6 **cups white flour**

Scald cornmeal, oats, salt, butter with 2$^1/_2$ cups boiling water. Mix well. Add scant cup of molasses. Dissolve 1 tablespoon (or one packet) yeast in $^1/_2$ cup warm water. When ready, add to above mixture. Mix. Add 6 cups white flour. Knead. Let rise 2 hours in mixing bowl. Then spoon into 2 greased loaf pans. Cover and let rise until double. Bake at 350°F. for one hour.

Brush top with butter and turn onto racks to cool. Yield: 2 loaves.

★*Beverley McInnes*

MARY MOORE'S STAFF OF LIFE

A friend (not Mary Moore) gave me this recipe years ago, and I have been making it ever since. It is the best bread I have ever tasted — particularly when still warm and fresh out of the oven. Thank you Mary Moore — wherever you are!

3 packages of yeast	$1/_2$ cup sunflower seeds or pieces
1 cup warm water (first amount)	5 tablespoons cooking oil
$1/_3$ cup molasses	$6^1/_2$ cups warm water
3 cups rolled oats	1 tablespoon salt
$1^1/_2$ cups boiling water	4 cups all-purpose flour (first amount)
1 cup cornmeal	approximately 3 cups all-purpose flour (second amount)
5 cups whole wheat flour	
1 cup rye flour	
$1/_2$ cup bran	

In a small bowl, soak yeast, warm water and molasses for 10 minutes. In a pot stir the 3 cups rolled oats into $1^1/_2$ cups boiling water for 2 to 3 minutes. Remove from heat.

Into a very large bowl measure cornmeal, whole wheat, rye flour, bran, sunflower seeds, oil, water, salt and 4 cups all-purpose flour and mix thoroughly. Add yeast and oat mixtures and stir like crazy until your arm has had it. Scrape down the sides of the bowl, cover and let rise until it doubles (about one hour). Sprinkle a large kneading area with 2 cups of all-purpose flour. Turn dough out onto it. Sprinkle top of dough with one more cup of flour and knead. It will be sticky and you must knead nearly all the flour in. This will take about 200 kneads, or about 10 minutes steady kneading. Shape the dough into a long roll. Cut into 5 even pieces. Roll out with a rolling pin and then roll up like a jelly roll and place in $8^1/_2$ x $4^1/_2$ x $2^1/_2$ inch pans tucking in all the folded ends. Brush tops with melted margarine or oil; cover and let rise until nearly one inch over rims. Do not allow them to overrise. Bake at 375°F. about 35-40 minutes. Cool on racks. Makes 5 loaves.

Note: Bread can be frozen after forming into the individual loaves. A loaf takes about 6 hours after being frozen to unthaw and rise one inch over the rim of the pan.

★ *Valda Ondaatje*

OLD-FASHIONED ROLLS

These rolls freeze well. I also make this recipe in the Cusinart — definitely the old and new here!

Bake the whole batch at once, or pinch off enough for lunch.

1	cup boiling water	4	cups white flour
1/4	cup sugar	1	packet or 1 cake yeast
1	tablespoon shortening or butter	1	teaspoon salt
		1	egg, beaten

Mix boiling water, sugar, salt and shortening. Cool until lukewarm. Add yeast, having dissolved it in $^{1}/_{2}$ cup warm water with pinch of sugar. Add beaten egg. Stir in 2 cups flour, and then the remaining flour.

Cover and let stand in buttered bowl in refrigerator. (One week-10 days sufficient refrigerator life.) Shape into rolls, put in buttered pan, cover and let double in size. Bake at 400°F. for 15 to 20 minutes. Brush tops with butter and let cool on racks.

★ *Beverley McInnes*

BROWN BREAD

An easy-to-make bread. Oatmeal and molasses are traditionally Nova Scotian additions to many bread recipes.

2   cups boiling water
1   tablespoon salt
$^1/_2$ cup molasses
4 or 5 cups flour

1   package yeast dissolved in
    $^1/_2$ cup warm water and 1
    teaspoon sugar
1   cup oatmeal
1   tablespoon margarine

Add boiling water to oats, salt and margarine. Let stand until lukewarm. Add molasses, yeast, flour. Knead well and let rise to double in bulk. Put in pans, let raise again. Bake at 375°F. for 45 minutes. Yield: 2 loaves.

★*Una Redden*

HEALTH BREAD

Dates or raisins can be added for extra flavour.

1   cup sifted white flour
2   cups whole wheat flour
1   teaspoon salt
$^1/_2$ cup sugar

1   teaspoon soda
$1^1/_2$ cups milk
$^1/_2$ cup molasses

Mix together flour, salt and sugar. Dissolve soda in the milk and add the molasses. Add liquids to dry ingredients and mix thoroughly. Pour into greased pan and bake slowly for $1^1/_2$ hours at 325°F. Yield: 1 loaf.

★*Leta Udall*

BRAN MUFFINS

Batter is made ahead of time and is stored in refrigerator — so easy to have warm, moist muffins for breakfast — all you do is bake them!

2	cups All Bran	$1^1/_2$	teaspoons salt
2	cups boiling water	4	eggs
1	cup shortening	1	quart buttermilk
$2^1/_2$	cups sugar	4	cups Bran Buds or 100%
5	cups flour		Nabisco bran
5	teaspoons soda	1	pound raisins

Combine everything until moist. Store batter in a covered container in fridge. Makes 1 gallon. Will keep at least 6 weeks in fridge. Bake at 375°F. for 20 minutes.

★*Jill Flinn*

WHOLE GRAIN MUFFINS

This recipe makes a very tender, moist muffin — and it's good for you, too!

2	cups whole wheat flour	1	cup bran
$1/_8$	teaspoon salt	$1/_4$	cup oil
$1/_4$	cup powdered skim milk	$1/_3$	cup honey
3	teaspoons baking powder	1	cup milk

Sift together the flour, salt, powdered milk and baking powder. Add the remaining ingredients and mix. Bake in muffin tins at 400°F. for 12 to 15 minutes. Yield: 12 muffins.

★*Janet Ondaatje*

APPLESAUCE-DATE MUFFINS

This recipe makes very moist and tender muffins — and they freeze beautifully.

6	cups whole wheat flour	2	cups sugar
2	cups cracked wheat	6	eggs
2	cups wheat germ	3	cups oil
2	tablespoons baking soda	5^1/$_2$	cups milk
2	tablespoons salt	1	10-ounce can applesauce
		1	cup dates, chopped

Mix first 6 ingredients in large bowl. Mix all wet ingredients and dates in another bowl. Stir into dry mixture. Batter will be thin. Fill muffin tins approximately half full. Bake about 20 minutes in 350°F. oven.

★*Terry Kierans*

MISTRAL MUFFINS

Mistral Muffins provide all the wholesome energy that winning sailors need!

1	cup all-purpose flour	^{1}/$_2$	cup melted shortening
^{3}/$_4$	cup whole wheat flour	1	cup raisins
^{1}/$_4$	cup wheat germ	5	teaspoons baking powder
2	cups All Bran or Bran Buds cereal	1	teaspoon salt
2	cups milk	^{1}/$_2$	cup honey or molasses
2	eggs	2	teaspoons cinnamon
		1	teaspoon nutmeg

Combine All Bran and milk. Let mixture stand until most of the moisture is absorbed. Add eggs, shortening and honey; beat well.

Stir in raisins. Sift flour and wheat germ together. Add baking powder, salt, cinnamon and nutmeg. Combine dry ingredients with All Bran mixture, stirring only until combined. Fill greased muffin tins until $3/4$ full. Bake in a 400°F. oven for about 20-25 minutes. Serve hot! Yield: 24 muffins.

★*Gail Walker*

GOUGERE

A sort of cheese bread, gougère is delicious served hot with a main course salad for lunch or a light supper.

2	cups milk	8	eggs
$1/2$	cup butter	6	ounces Swiss cheese, finely cubed
2	teaspoons salt		milk
	pepper, to taste		
2	cups flour, sifted	2	tablespoons Swiss cheese, grated

Scald milk and let it cool. Put it in a largish saucepan and add cut-up butter, salt and pepper. Bring to a rolling boil and add flour, all at once. Cook over low heat, beating briskly with a wooden spoon, until mixture forms a ball. Remove from heat and beat in 8 eggs, one at a time. When shiny and smooth, mix in 6 ounces Swiss cheese. Let the dough cool.

Divide dough in half. With a soup spoon, scoop out from one half of the dough pieces the size of an egg. Place on buttered baking dish in a ring, leaving a space in the middle about $2^{1}/_{2}$ inches in diameter. Use teaspoon to make smaller ovals on top of first layer. Make another ring with remaining dough. Brush gougères with milk, and sprinkle each with remaining cheese. Bake at 375°F. for about 45 minutes until they are puffed and golden brown.

★*Valda Ondaatje*

PEGGY'S QUICK BISCUITS

The ingredients may be combined and stored in refrigerator until needed — then add ice water and bake.

1 cup flour	1 cup shredded or grated
1 tablespoon shortening	sharp Cheddar cheese
2 teaspoons baking powder	$1/2$ cup ice water

Work together first three ingredients. Add cheese. Add cold water quickly, and stir. Drop by spoonfuls on greased pan. Bake in pre-heated 400°F. oven for 10 minutes. Yield: 20-24 biscuits.

★*Elizabeth Pellow*

TEA BISCUITS

A family favorite, usually served with strawberry jam.

2 cups flour	4 tablespoons shortening
4 teaspoons baking powder	1 egg
$1/2$ teaspoon salt	$1/2$ cup milk
2 tablespoons sugar	

Sift flour, baking powder, salt and sugar together. Add shortening and mix in well with a fork. Beat egg slightly and add milk to make $3/4$ cup. Add to flour and blend lightly. Roll out to $1/2$-inch thickness; cut with floured biscuit cutter. Bake in a hot, 475°F., oven for 12 to 15 minutes.

★*Margaret Corkum*

PUMPKIN NUT BREAD

This is a good way of using up a Halloween pumpkin. Just scrape out the melted wax and charred area, chop into sections and peel. Then boil in a small amount of water until soft. Mash or purée the pulp.

1 cup butter or margarine	1 teaspoon baking soda
$2^1/_2$ cups sugar	1 teaspoon baking powder
3 eggs	1 teaspoon cinnamon
2 cups cooked pumpkin purée	1 teaspoon ground cloves
	$^1/_2$ teaspoon nutmeg
1 teaspoon vanilla extract	1 cup chopped walnuts
3 cups sifted flour	1 cup dark or golden raisins
1 teaspoon salt	

Cream butter and sugar. Beat in eggs one at a time. Add pumpkin and vanilla. Sift together the dry ingredients. Blend with pumpkin mixture. Add nuts and raisins.

Pour into two 9 x 5 x 3-inch greased loaf pans. Bake in a 350°F. oven for 60 to 70 minutes. Yield: 2 loaves.

Cream Cheese Icing

$^1/_4$ cup butter or margarine	$2^1/_2$ cups icing sugar
1 package (8 ounces) cream cheese	1 teaspoon vanilla

Beat together until soft enough to spread.

This bread, iced or plain, freezes very well.

★*Willa Creighton*

CRANBERRY BREAD

A very moist, decorative and delicious sweet bread.

2 cups flour	juice and rind of one orange
1$^1/_2$ tablespoons baking powder	2 tablespoons butter and boiling water
$^1/_2$ teaspoon salt	1 egg, beaten
$^1/_2$ teaspoon baking soda	1 cup chopped raw cranberries
1 cup white sugar	$^1/_2$ cup crushed walnuts

Put orange juice and rind in measuring cup, add butter, and fill to $^3/_4$ with boiling water. Add egg and mix well. Add dry ingredients. Mix all well. Fold in cranberries and nuts. Pour into greased loaf pan. Bake at 350°F. for 40 to 50 minutes. Yield: one loaf.

★*Terry Kierans*

PUMPKIN LOAF

Wonderful when still warm with lots of butter.

1$^1/_2$ cups flour	2 eggs
1 teaspoon baking powder	$^3/_4$ cup cooking oil
1 teaspoon baking soda	1 cup raisins, dates, or nuts
2 teaspoons cinnamon	$^3/_4$ cup pumpkin, mashed
1 cup white sugar	

Sift together flour, baking powder, baking soda, sugar and cinnamon three times. Combine with the rest of the ingredients and pour into a greased loaf pan and bake at 350°F. for about 1 hour. Yield: 1 loaf.

★*Betty L. Bezanson*

BANANA NUT BREAD

This bread goes well with a fresh fruit salad.

$1^1/_2$ cups sugar
1 cup butter
2 eggs
3 cups sifted flour
$^1/_2$ cup sour milk

$1^1/_2$ teaspoons baking soda
 pinch of salt
3 ripe bananas
1 cup chopped pecans

Cream the sugar and butter together. Add 2 eggs, one at a time alternately with the flour. Mix the soda and salt with the sour milk and then add to the egg and flour mixture. Mash the bananas and add to the mixture. Bake in greased loaf pans in moderate oven (350°F.). Test for doneness in center of loaf with cake tester after 40 or 50 minutes. Yield: 2 loaves.

★*Alberta Pew*

LEMON BREAD

This is my grandmother's recipe — as good today as when she baked it.

1 cup white sugar
6 tablespoons butter
2 eggs, well beaten
$^1/_2$ cup white flour
$1^1/_2$ teaspoons baking
 powder

$^1/_2$ teaspoon salt
$^1/_2$ cup milk
 grated rind of 1 lemon
$^1/_2$ cup chopped nuts
 juice of 1 lemon mixed with
 $^1/_3$ cup white sugar

Mix all ingredients together (except lemon juice mixed with white sugar) and beat well. Pour into greased loaf pan and bake at

350°F. for 1 hour. Take out of oven and immediately pour sweetened lemon juice over bread. Let set for 10 minutes before taking bread out of pan.

★*Edith Webber*

WHOLE WHEAT PASTRY

Devised one wintry day in desperation when I discovered I didn't have enough white flour!

1¹/₂ **cups whole wheat flour**	1 **pound shortening**
1¹/₂ **cups all-purpose flour**	1 **teaspoon salt**
¹/₂ **cup bran flour or cereal**	1¹/₂ **teaspoons baking powder**
powder	1 **egg**
¹/₂ **cup wheat germ**	1 **cup cold water**
¹/₂ **cup instant rolled oats**	

Beat egg in water thoroughly. Combine dry ingredients. Cut in shortening. Stir in egg-water mixture. Stir with a fork, but you may have to use your hands to finish the mixing. Dough feels wet, but this allows you to use more flour while rolling out. This mixture will make enough dough for three 2-crust pies or six single-layer pies. It can be used with your favourite recipes, but is especially tasty with fruit fillings.

★*Gail Walker*

QUICK AND DELICIOUS DOUGHNUTS

A favourite family recipe, these doughnuts really are quick and delicious.

$^1/_2$ **cup butter or shortening**
1 cup sugar
2 eggs
1 teaspoon grated lemon rind
$4^1/_2$ **cups sifted all purpose flour (I use 1 cup whole wheat for improved health and flavour)**

2 teaspoons baking powder
2 teaspoons nutmeg or less, according to taste
1 cup milk
sifted confectioners' sugar

Beat butter, sugar, eggs and lemon rind until fluffy. Resift flour with baking powder, salt and nutmeg. Add to beaten mixture in small amounts, alternately with additions of milk. Blend each addition in well. Turn dough out on floured surface and roll to about $^1/_3$ inch thickness. Cut with doughnut cutter. Do not re-roll leftover bits. Fry them as they are. Have deep fat heated to 365°F. Drop doughnuts in, a few at a time so you don't lower heat of fat. Fry until brown on one side. Turn, brown other. Takes about 3 minutes. Strain out, let drain on absorbent paper. Dip in confectioners' sugar. Yield: 2 dozen.

★*Bertie Baker*

Cakes and Cookies

CARROT CAKE

Delicious with a mid-morning cup of coffee!

4 eggs	1 teaspoon cinnamon
$1^1/_2$ cups sugar or part honey	1 teaspoon ginger
1 cup vegetable oil	2 teaspoons baking soda
2 cups grated raw carrots	$^1/_2$ teaspoon salt
$1^1/_2$ cups flour, white, wholewheat or a mixture	1 cup chopped nuts (optional)
$^1/_2$ cup wheat germ	

Beat eggs, add sugar, oil and grated carrots. Mix well after each addition. In a separate bowl, mix flour, spices, soda and salt. Add to batter and beat for 3 minutes. Add nuts and wheat germ. Bake at 350°F. for 35 minutes in two 9-inch layer pans or for 45 minutes or in one $9x13x1^1/_2$-inch pan.

Cream Cheese Icing

6 ounces cream cheese	2 - 3 cups icing sugar
6 tablespoons margarine	1 teaspoon vanilla

Let the cheese and margarine soften. Add sugar and vanilla. Mix well.

★*Hilda Tzagarakis*

COFFEE CAKE

A cinnamon-flavoured cake goes well with morning coffee.

2 cups sifted flour	1 cup milk
1¹/₂ cups sugar	3 tablespoons baking powder
³/₄ cup shortening	salt
2 eggs	cinnamon, to taste

Sift together flour, sugar and shortening. Mix with fingers until fine. Take out 1 cup. To the remainder add the eggs, milk, baking powder and salt. To mixture taken out, add cinnamon to taste and sprinkle on top of batter, before baking 30 minutes at 350°F.

★*Alberta Pew*

LEMON REFRIGERATOR CAKE

Excellent for a luncheon or a dinner party.

6 eggs	whipped cream
³/₄ cup granulated sugar	maraschino cherries
juice and rind of 1¹/₂ lemons	lady fingers (about 2 bags bought)
6 tablespoons boiling water	large mould with removable bottom
1 package plain gelatin dissolved in ¹/₂ cup cold water	

Beat egg yolks until lemon coloured. Slowly add ¹/₂ of the sugar, lemon juice (all) and rind. Mix well. Slowly add boiling water. Cook in double boiler until thick. Remove from stove and add dissolved gelatin. Cool. Beat egg whites until stiff, adding rest of sugar gradually. Then add to cooled custard. Just fold in. Line mould with lady fingers cutting off one end of each to crush and scatter on bottom — stand them straight — around mould and pour batter mixture into mould — carefully so as not to knock lady fingers over.

Leave in refrigerator overnight. Serve with whipped cream, and decorate with cut maraschino cherries.

★*Terry Kierans*

DOUBLE PISTACHIO CAKE

A boon for the busy cook.

1 **package (2-layer size) yellow cake mix**	3 **eggs**
1 **package (4-serving size) Jello Pistachio Flavour Instant Pudding and Pie Filling**	1 **cup club soda or water**
	$^1/_2$ **cup oil**
	$^1/_2$ **cup chopped nuts**

Combine all ingredients in large bowl. Blend; then beat at medium speed of electric mixer for 2 minutes. Pour into 2 greased and floured 9" layer pans or one bundt pan. Bake at 350°F. for 30-35 minutes. Cool in pan 15 minutes. Remove. Cool on rack.

Pistachio Fluffy Frosting
Pour $1^1/_2$ cups cold milk; add 1 envelope Dream Whip and 1 package (4 ounce size) Pistachio Instant Pudding and Pie Filling. Beat slowly to blend. Increase beating speed to high and whip until mixture forms soft peaks (4-6 minutes). Makes 3 cups. Refrigerate cake immediately after frosting.

★*Dee Dee Blain*

HOT WATER GINGERBREAD

This gingerbread is especially good served warm with vanilla cream sauce. An ideal dessert with a light main course.

2 cups pastry flour, sifted once or 1 $^3/_4$ cups once-sifted all-purpose flour
2 teaspoons baking powder
$^1/_2$ teaspoon baking soda
$^1/_2$ teaspoon salt
1 teaspoon ground ginger
1 teaspoon ground cinnamon
1 teaspoon grated nutmeg

5 tablespoons shortening
$^3/_4$ cup lightly packed brown sugar
$^1/_4$ cup molasses
2 eggs, well beaten
$^1/_2$ teaspoon grated lemon rind
$^1/_2$ teaspoon vanilla
$^3/_4$ cup boiling water

Grease an 8-inch square cake pan and line bottom with greased paper. Preheat oven to 325°F. Sift flour, baking powder, baking soda, salt, ginger, cinnamon and nutmeg together 3 times. Cream shortening, gradually blend in sugar. Add molasses and well beaten eggs, part at a time, beating well after each addition. Stir in lemon and vanilla. Add flour mixture to cream mixture, about $^1/_3$ at a time, combining lightly after each addition. Gently stir in boiling water. Turn into prepared pan. Bake in oven for 45 minutes.

Vanilla Cream Sauce

1$^1/_2$ cups milk
3 tablespoons flour
$^1/_3$ cup granulated sugar

few grains of salt
1 tablespoon butter or margarine
$^1/_2$ teaspoon vanilla

Scald milk in a double boiler. Combine flour, sugar and salt in a small bowl. Slowly stir scalded milk into sugar mixture. Cook over boiling water, stirring constantly, for 2 minutes. Remove from heat and stir in butter or margarine and vanilla. Yield: 1$^1/_2$ cups of sauce.

★*Mrs. Cavell Stevens*

OLD FASHIONED GINGERBREAD

Old fashioned, but still very much in fashion!

1 **cup molasses**	1 **teaspoon ginger**
$^1/_2$ **cup butter or margarine**	1 **teaspoon cinnamon**
2$^1/_3$ **cups flour**	$^1/_4$ **teaspoon ground cloves**
pinch of salt	1 **cup sour cream**
$^3/_4$ **teaspoon baking soda**	

Put molasses and butter or margarine in a pan and heat to boiling. Sift dry ingredients. When butter and molasses have cooled slightly, add sour cream, and then stir in dry ingredients. Pour into a buttered loaf pan (9 x 5 x 3) and bake at 350°F. for about 40 minutes.

Serve warm with whipped cream, or, topped with a spoonful of vanilla ice cream and covered with the easiest and best chocolate sauce:

$^1/_4$ **cup butter**	$^1/_4$ **cup water**
$^1/_4$ **cup cocoa**	1 **cup sugar**

Mix together in a pan. Bring to a boil and boil slowly for about 3 minutes.

★*Willa Creighton*

PAT'S GINGERBREAD

This gingerbread freezes well, but also keeps moist unfrozen. I serve it with hot lemon sauce.

$2^1/_2$ cups flour
1 teaspoon cinnamon
2 teaspoons ginger
   pinch each of allspice,
   cloves, mace
$3/_4$ cup brown sugar
$1^1/_2$ cups molasses

2 teaspoons baking soda, dissolved in $1/_4$ cup boiling water; filling cup up with milk
1 egg
$1/_2$ cup oil

Sift flour and spices. Add sugar, molasses, baking soda, egg and oil. Mix to combine, and bake at 325°F. for 45 to 55 minutes. This makes two 8x8x2-inch gingerbreads.

★*Sheila M.L. Campbell*

CHOCOLATE CAKE WITH BEETS

This combination must be tried — a unique mixture of flavours and ingredients.

$1^1/_2$ cups sugar
1 cup cooking oil
3 eggs, beaten
$1^1/_2$ cups sieved beets, cooked
2 squares melted chocolate

$1^3/_4$ cups all purpose flour, sifted
$1^1/_2$ teaspoons baking soda
$1/_4$ teaspoon salt
$1/_4$ teaspoon vanilla

Combine eggs and sugar. Add oil, beets and flour. Stir well. Add soda, salt and vanilla. Bake at 350°F. for 50 to 60 minutes.

★*Debbie Verspaget*

COCONUT COCOA CAKE

Coconut and cocoa go well together.

$1^7/_8$ cups flour
$1^1/_2$ cups sugar
$1^1/_4$ teaspoons baking powder
$1/_2$ teaspoon baking soda
$1/_2$ cup shredded coconut

6   tablespoons cocoa
$2/_3$ cup shortening
1   cup sour milk
2   eggs

Sift together flour, sugar, baking powder, soda and cocoa. Add shortening and sour milk, and beat for 2 minutes. Add eggs and coconut, and beat for 2 more minutes. Pour into two 8-inch round cake pans and bake in a 350°F. oven. Frost as desired.

★Thirsty Thinkers Tea Room

MARY YOUNG'S WHITE FRUIT CAKE

A moist, flavourful cake with good keeping qualities.

$2/_3$ cup butter
2   cups white sugar
3   eggs
1   cup milk
3   cups flour
2   teaspoons baking powder
$1/_4$ teaspoon salt
$1/_2$ pound pineapple

$1/_2$ pound mixed fruit
1   pound red and green cherries
1   pound white raisins
$1/_2$ cup flour (to flour the fruit)
$1/_4$ pound coconut (diced)
1   teaspoon vanilla
1   teaspoon lemon extract

Cream butter and sugar well; add well-beaten eggs, milk and flour alternately; beat well; add floured fruit; mix. Bake in a 300°F. oven for $1^3/_4$ hours.

★Evelyn Stevens

WAR CAKE

This recipe was made for me by the late Sarah Graves. We took it on a 3-week cruise to Newfoundland and it became better after it had been kept for a while — as do all fruit cakes. An almost identical recipe is in one of Emily Lynton's cook books, called "Canada's War Cake." These cook books date from before 1920, so it must have been created during World War I. Emily Lynton was my mother's, Queenie Brookfield's, nurse and afterwards reigned in Grandfather's kitchen at Glen Cove, Chester, until her death. She let me range in her kitchen at will and gave me my first cooking lessons.

2 cups brown sugar	2 tablespoons shortening
1¹/₂ teaspoons salt	2 cups cold water
1 teaspoon cinnamon	1 pound raisins, any kind
¹/₂ teaspoon cloves	3 cups flour
	1 heaping teaspoon baking soda

Combine first 7 ingredients and boil for 5 minutes. When cool, add flour sifted with baking soda. Mix well and bake for 1¹/₄ hours at 350°F.

★*Marian Straus*

MOLASSES COOKIES

This is my husband's grandmother's recipe. It is about one hundred years old. He says that he has eaten a barrel full of these cookies over the last forty years, and he is still hale and hearty!

1	cup sugar	1	teaspoon salt
1	egg, beaten	1	teaspoon cinnamon
1	cup melted shortening	1	teaspoon cloves
4	cups flour	$^1/_2$	cup hot water, mixed with
		1	teaspoon soda

Mix ingredients. Chill overnight. When ready to use, roll and bake at 350°F. for about 15 minutes.

★*Iris J. Wagner*

BUTTER COOKIES

This is an old German recipe given to me by Ella Bauerle and is marvelous at Christmastime, decorated with coloured sugar or brushed with egg white, with almonds in the centre.

1	pound butter	3	large or 4 small eggs
1	pound sugar (2 cups)	$^1/_2$	teaspoon baking powder
1	pound flour (4 cups)		grated rind of 1 lemon

Cream butter and sugar. Add eggs and lemon rind. Then add flour and baking powder, sifted together. Chill dough. When ready to use, roll thin and cut into any shape desired. Bake at 375°F. for 8 to 12 minutes.

★*Bertie Baker*

OATMEAL RAISIN COOKIES

These nutritious cookies are ideal for hungry children when they come home from school.

$^3/_4$ cup raisins
1$^1/_2$ cups rolled oats
$^3/_4$ cup brown sugar, firmly packed
$^1/_2$ cup melted shortening, cooled
1 egg, slightly beaten

$^3/_4$ cup sifted flour
1$^1/_2$ teaspoons baking powder
$^3/_4$ teaspoon salt
$^1/_4$ teaspoon maple flavouring

Rinse raisins and drain. Combine oats and sugar. Stir in shortening and egg. Sift together flour, baking powder and salt. Add to first mixture. Stir in maple flavouring and raisins. Drop by teaspoons onto greased cookie sheet. Bake in hot oven (400°F.) for 8 to 10 minutes. Remove to wire rack to cool. Makes 3 dozen cookies.

★Olive G. Dorey

DATE CRUMBLE

This is a very large recipe, but it can be halved.

4 eggs
2 cups sugar
2 tablespoons flour

4 teaspoons baking powder
2 cups chopped walnuts
2 cups chopped dates

Mix together, and spread on 4 buttered pie tins. Bake in slow oven (275°F.) for 45 minutes. Crumble into small pieces and mix with whipped cream.

★Constance B. McInnes

GINGER COOKIES

Good any time of year, but in great demand at Christmas time.

$^3/_4$ **cup shortening**	2 **cups flour**
1 **cup white sugar**	2 **teaspoons soda**
1 **egg**	$^1/_2$ **teaspoon salt**
$^1/_4$ **cup molasses**	1 **teaspoon ginger**

Mix in the given order. Roll batter into balls and then dip in sugar. Press with fork. Put cookies on a buttered cookie sheet and bake for 8-10 minutes in a 400°F. oven.

★*Hilda Tzagarakis*

EASY FILLED DATE COOKIES

Moist and flavourful, these date cookies never last long at our house.

Batter

1 **cup shortening**	$3^1/_2$ **cups flour**
2 **cups brown sugar**	$^1/_2$ **teaspoon salt**
2 **or 3 eggs, depending on size**	1 **teaspoon baking soda**
	$^1/_8$ **teaspoon cinnamon**
$^1/_2$ **cup warm water**	
1 **teaspoon vanilla**	

Filling

2 **cups dates**	$^3/_4$ **cup water**
$^3/_4$ **cup sugar**	

Mix in order given. Deposit batter on the greased cookie sheet by teaspoonfuls; add $^1/_2$ teaspoon date mixture. Cover date mixture with $^1/_2$ teaspoon of the cookie mixture. Bake at 400°F. for 10 to 12 minutes.

★*Betty L. Bezanson*

MERINGUE COOKIES

Chocolate lovers can celebrate with these chocolate meringues.

3   egg whites
$^1/_8$ teaspoon salt
$^1/_2$ teaspoon cream of tartar

$^3/_4$ cup sugar
6   ounces semisweet chocolate
    morsels
$^3/_4$ cup nuts, coarsely chopped

Beat egg whites in a large bowl. When foamy, add salt and cream of tartar. When stiff, beat in sugar. Stir in chocolate morsels and nuts. Drop batter by teaspoonfuls onto a cookie sheet lined with buttered wax paper dusted with flour. Bake in a preheated 200°F. oven for at least 1 hour. Shut off oven and let cookies dry several hours or overnight. Makes about 7 dozen cookies.

★*Valda Ondaatje*

HONEY NUTTERS

A superb snack, and great on picnics.

1   cup crunchy peanut
    butter
$^2/_3$ cup honey
$^1/_2$ cup instant milk powder

16 graham crackers
1   cup coconut or toasted
    wheat germ

Combine peanut butter, honey and milk. Stir until blended. Crush graham crackers and add to the mixture. Mix by hand until well blended. Roll into balls, then roll in coconut or wheat germ.

★*Hilda Tzagarakis*

KRINKLES

A popular regional sweet — easy to make and good tasting.

$^3/_4$ **cup butter**
$^3/_4$ **cup brown sugar**
$^3/_4$ **cup white flour**
$^3/_4$ **cup rolled oats**

$^1/_2$ **cup coconut**
pinch of salt
$^1/_2$ **teaspoon baking soda,**
dissolved in 1 tablespoon
hot water

Mix everything together. Roll in small balls, press down with a fork and bake on a cookie sheet at 350°F. until browned at the edges.

★*Edith Webber*

LADY FINGERS

Wonderful with homemade vanilla ice cream.

1 **cup butter**
$^3/_4$ **cup brown sugar**
1 **teaspoon vanilla**
1 **whole egg and 1 yolk**
(save white for whipping)
2 **cups flour**

1 **teaspoon salt**
$^1/_8$ **teaspoon baking soda**
1 **cup rolled oats**
1 **cup chopped nuts**
jam

Combine butter, sugar, vanilla, eggs, flour, salt, water, baking soda and rolled oats in a large bowl. Shape dough into fingers and dip into whipped egg white. Roll fingers in chopped nuts. Make a depression into fingers and bake for 5 minutes in a 350°F. oven. Take from oven and make the depression deeper (so jam won't run out). Bake about 15 minutes more or until fingers are brown. When done, fill depression with jam.

★*Elaine Heisler*

PEANUT BUTTER BALLS

These peanut butter balls require no baking and are extremely nutritious.

1 cup crunchy peanut butter	$^1/_4$ cup sesame or sunflower seeds
$^1/_2$ cup milk powder	$^1/_8$ cup wheat germ
$^1/_2$ cup raisins	$^1/_8$ - $^1/_4$ cup honey

Mix all the ingredients until thoroughly blended. Roll in wheat germ or coconut. Store in refrigerator or a tight container.

★*Hilda Tzagarakis*

IRRESISTIBLE CHOCOLATE SQUARES

And they are, too!

$^1/_3$ cup butter or margarine	$^1/_2$ package chocolate chips
1$^1/_2$ cups brown sugar	nuts
2 eggs, separated	few grains salt
1 cup flour	red and green cherries
1 teaspoon baking powder	1 cup coconut, shredded

Mix $^1/_2$ cup brown sugar and butter. Add the egg yolks, baking powder and salt. Put it in an 8x8-inch pan and pat down. Sprinkle with chocolate chips, a few nuts, and red and green sweet cherries. Beat the egg whites. Fold in the rest of the brown sugar and coconut. Spread over other mixture and bake at 325°F. for 35 minutes. Cool, then cut into squares.

★*Connie Stevens*

COCONUT BUTTERSCOTCH SQUARES

One of our very favourite sweets. Wonderful with a fresh cup of coffee.

1 cup flour	1 cup sugar
1 teaspoon salt	1 egg, slightly beaten
1 teaspoon baking powder	2 tablespoons melted butter
milk	

Add enough milk to egg and melted butter so that there is one cup of liquid. Make a well in the dry ingredients and add the liquid. Mix well. Pour into an 8x8-inch pan and bake in a 350°F. oven for 20 to 25 minutes.

Topping

2 tablespoons cream or canned milk	$^1/_2$ cup brown sugar
pinch of salt	$^1/_2$ cup coconut
	3 tablespoons melted butter

Combine ingredients and cook until mixture comes to a boil, stirring constantly. Remove from heat and spread on top of baked bottom. Return to 425°F. oven and bake for 5 to 7 minutes.

★*Thirsty Thinkers Tea Room*

LEMON SQUARES

Delectable! For orange squares, substitute oranges.

$1/2$ **cup margarine**	**1 cup flour**
$1/4$ **teaspoon salt**	**2 tablespoons brown sugar**

Mix, and press into 8" x 8" pan; bake 10 minutes at 350°F.

Top

2 eggs	$1^1/_2$ **cups coconut**
2 teaspoons flour	**juice and rind of one lemon**
1 cup white sugar	

Mix, and spread on first mixture. Bake 20 minutes at 350°F.

Ice with lemon icing.

Lemon Icing

$1/4$ **cup margarine**	**juice of one lemon**
	icing sugar

Mix and add icing sugar to desired consistency.

★*Mona Campbell*

GOOD MOLASSES COOKIES

Sugar sprinkled on cookies before baking adds a decorative touch.

1 cup shortening	**4 cups flour**
1 cup sugar	**1 teaspoon cinnamon**
1 cup molasses	**1 teaspoon ginger**
2 teaspoons baking soda dissolved in $1/2$ cup warm water	$1/2$ **teaspoon cloves**

Combine all ingredients and cool in refrigerator for 1 hour before cooking. Roll in balls and flatten with a fork. Bake at 350°F. for 8 to 10 minutes.

★*Betty L. Bezanson*

PEANUT BUTTER EASTER EGGS

A creation that is as appealing as an Easter bonnet.

$^1/_2$ cup corn syrup
$^3/_4$ cup peanut butter
$^1/_4$ cup soft butter
$^1/_2$ teaspoon salt

1 teaspoon vanilla
4 cups icing sugar
$^3/_4$ cup peanuts (crushed)
melted chocolate

Blend all but sugar and nuts. Beat in sugar. Knead until well blended and work in crushed peanuts.

Shape into eggs. Chill until firm. Dip in melted chocolate and decorate as you wish.

★*Margaret Pulsifer*

MOM'S SUGAR COOKIES

A traditional favourite, as good today as a hundred years ago.

1 cup shortening
1 cup granulated sugar
2 eggs
2 teaspoons vanilla

1 teaspoon cream of tartar
$2^1/_2$ cups sifted all-purpose flour
1 teaspoon salt
fine sugar

Blend shortening and sugar. Add eggs and vanilla and beat thoroughly. Blend in sifted dry ingredients. On lightly floured board, pat or roll out dough to $^1/_4$ inch thickness. Cut into 3-inch rounds and arrange on greased cookie sheet. Sprinkle with fine sugar. Bake at 375°F. for 8 to 10 minutes. Cool slightly.

★*Roxanne Udall*

DEBBY PIERS' FUDGE

A wonderful old family recipe — with tremendous gift-giving possibilities!

2 pounds light brown sugar	**1 pinch cream of tartar**
1 cup milk	**1 teaspoon vanilla**
3$^1/_2$ tablespoons butter	**$^3/_4$ cup chopped nuts**
1 pinch salt	

Combine sugar, milk, 2 tablespoons of the butter, salt and cream of tartar in a heavy saucepan. Mix with wooden spoon over high heat; reduce to medium heat when butter melts. Boil for about 20 minutes, stirring sides and bottom from time to time. Test in cold water until a firm ball is formed.

Let cool for 20 minutes. Add 1 teaspoon vanilla, 1$^1/_2$ tablespoons butter, $^3/_4$ cup chopped nuts. Beat for about 5 minutes until it start to stiffen.

Pour into pan smeared with butter. Etch squares and cut before hardening.

★ *Desmond Piers*

Desserts

BLACKBERRY PUDDING

In Nova Scotia in late summer, blackberries are everywhere, and one cannot step off a country path without encountering these beautiful, dark, shiny berries.

$^1/_2$ cup water
$^1/_4$ cup sugar
2$^1/_2$ cups picked-over
    blackberries

thin slices of stale white
bread
whipped cream

In a stainless steel or enameled saucepan combine water and sugar, bring the water to a boil over moderate heat, stirring, and boil the syrup, undisturbed, for 5 minutes. Add blackberries and simmer the mixture, covered, for 15 minutes, or until the berries are soft. Strain the mixture through a fine sieve into a bowl, reserving the pulp. Line a deep 1-quart soufflé dish with very thin slices of stale white bread, crusts removed, and drizzle the bread with $^1/_4$ cup of the juice. Spread half the reserved pulp over the bread and cover it with very thin slices of stale white bread, crusts removed. Spread the remaining pulp over the bread, cover it with very thin slices of white bread, crusts removed, and drizzle the remaining juice over the pudding. Invert a small plate just large enough to fit inside the dish over the pudding, set a 3-pound weight on it, and chill the pudding overnight. Remove the weight and plate, invert a serving plate over the pudding and invert the pudding onto the plate. Serve the pudding with whipped cream or crème fraîche. Serves 4.

★ *Janet Ondaatje*

MAPLE SYRUP PUDDING

In the early spring in Chester every home that boasts a maple tree on its lawn has a can hanging from it to catch the sap for making maple syrup.

2$^1/_2$ tablespoons cornstarch	$^2/_3$ cup powdered milk
2 cups water	$^1/_4$ cup maple syrup

Combine everything in a jar and shake until all ingredients are dissolved and mixture is foamy. Cook in double boiler until thick. Pour into a serving dish and refrigerate until cold.

★ *Grace McClung*

BLUEBERRY YUM

Serve warm or cold. Truly a treat.

2 quarts blueberries, fresh or frozen	lemon juice, $^1/_2$ or whole lemon depending on sweetness of berries
2 tablespoons arrowroot flour	
$^1/_4$ cup brown sugar, or more if berries are sour	

Butter shallow baking pan. Mix flour and sugar with berries. Put in pan. Sprinkle with lemon juice. Preheat oven to 350°F.

Topping

$^1/_2$ cup flour	1 teaspoon cinnamon
$^1/_2$ cup oatmeal	$^1/_2$ teaspoon nutmeg
$^3/_4$ cup brown sugar	$^1/_3$ cup butter

Mix until crumbly.

Spread topping over blueberries in pan. Pat evenly over berries. Bake for 35 minutes or until berries bubble. Serves 6.

★ *Bertie Baker*

BLUEBERRY BUCKLE

One of our favourite recipes, we hope that others will enjoy this dessert as much as our friends and we do. Other fruit, such as apples or peaches, may be substituted for the blueberries, but we prefer it with blueberries.

Batter	Topping
$^1/_4$ **cup butter**	$^1/_4$ **cup butter**
1 **cup flour**	$^1/_2$ **cup brown sugar**
$^1/_2$ **cup sugar**	$^1/_3$ **cup flour**
$1^1/_2$ **teaspoons baking powder**	1 **teaspoon cinnamon, or,**
1 **egg**	**to taste**
pinch of salt	
$^1/_2$ **cup milk**	
2 **cups blueberries**	

Preheat oven to 400°F. Combine batter ingredients. Pour into greased 8" x 8" baking pan. Cover with berries. Combine topping ingredients and mix until mixture resembles coarse meal. Sprinkle over blueberries and bake for 45 minutes. Cool, slightly, cut in squares, and serve warm with vanilla ice cream or plain or whipped cream. Serves 9. May be frozen.

★*Dorothy Page Curry*

SWEDISH CREME WITH HOT BLUEBERRY SAUCE

This is one of our family's favourite ways of enjoying Nova Scotia blueberries.

1 cup heavy cream	1 cup sour cream
$1/_2$ cup sugar	$1/_2$ teaspoon vanilla
$1/_2$ tablespoon ($1/_2$ envelope) gelatin	

Mix heavy cream, sugar and gelatin in small saucepan. Set over low heat and heat, stirring until gelatin has completely dissolved (until grainy appearance is gone). Remove from heat and allow to cool until just slightly thickened and about room temperature. Carefully fold in sour cream and vanilla.

Chill 1 to 2 hours until firm. Serves 4. Doubles easily.

★*Lu Ann Polk*

HOT BLUEBERRY SAUCE

This keeps well in the refrigerator and can be reheated as needed.

2 cups blueberries	1 tablespoon lemon juice
$1/_2$ cup sugar	1 teaspoon cornstarch

In saucepan, heat blueberries with sugar and lemon juice in $1/_2$ cup water. Bring to boil and let boil 2 minutes. Boil 4 to 5 minutes longer if too watery. Taste for sugar.

Dissolve cornstarch in $1/_2$ cup cold water. Add to berries and boil another minute.

★*Lu Ann Polk*

IMPOSSIBLE PIE

Impossibly delicious!

4 eggs	**1 cup sugar**
$^1/_2$ cup margarine	**1 cup coconut**
$^1/_2$ cup flour	**vanilla**
2 cups milk	**$^1/_4$ teaspoon nutmeg, if desired**

Mix all ingredients in a blender or by hand. Pour into greased 10-inch pie plate. Bake at 350°F. for approximately 1 hour or until centre is firm. Serves 6.

★ *Betty L. Bezanson*

INSTANT BERRY ICE CREAM

A quick and fresh-tasting ice cream made in seconds in the food processor. Best prepared just before serving.

1 cup whipping cream	**1 pound unsweetened frozen**
$^1/_3$ cup sugar	**berries (strawberries,**
	blackberries, blueberries,
	cherries, etc.)

Place cream and sugar in food processor with steel knife and blend until thickened. Add frozen fruit a few pieces at a time and blend until smooth. Serve immediately. Serves 6.

★ *Valda Ondaatje*

RHUBARB CUSTARD PIE

So good!

2¹/₂ cups cut up rhubarb
2 egg yolks
2 egg whites
1 cup sugar

2 tablespoons flour
2 tablespoons melted butter
1 unbaked pastry shell

Beat egg yolks until thick, add sugar, flour, butter and rhubarb. Mix well. Pour into unbaked pastry shell and bake at 350°F. for 20 to 30 minutes. When baked, top with meringue made of the egg whites and a little sugar. If desired, this pie may be baked between two crusts.

★Margaret Corkum

FROZEN COLONIAL RUM PIE

This is also good served in individual dishes without the crust.

9-inch baked pie shell or crumb crust
1 envelope unflavoured gelatin
¹/₄ cup cold water

1¹/₃ cups sweetened condensed milk
¹/₄ cup dark rum
1 cup whipping cream

Dissolve the gelatin in the cold water. Add the condensed milk, rum and whipping cream. Mix ingredients and pour into pie shell. Freeze. Serves 6.

★Mrs. Dale Barkhouse

FROZEN CHEESECAKE

A little effort but worth every delicious calorie.

Crust

1¹/₄ cups crushed graham crackers
4 tablespoons chopped nuts
2 tablespoons sugar
1 teaspoon lemon peel
¹/₂ cup melted butter

Combine and press into a 9-inch springform pan. Bake at 350°F. for 10 minutes. Cool.

Filling

3 (8-ounce) packages of cream cheese
1 cup sugar
1 teaspoon vanilla
3 tablespoons lemon juice
1 teaspoon lemon rind
4 eggs

Beat cheese and add sugar gradually. Add vanilla, lemon juice, and lemon rind. Add eggs one at a time and beat at medium speed 10 minutes until fluffy. Pour into pan over crust and bake at 250°F. for 35 minutes. Turn off the heat and cool for 30 minutes in the oven with the door open.

Topping

1 pint sour cream
¹/₂ pint sugar
1 teaspoon vanilla
cinnamon to taste

Combine and whip for 10 minutes until foamy. Spoon over the top of the cheesecake and bake at 250°F. for 10 minutes. Sprinkle with cinnamon. Cool, wrap, and freeze. Take out of freezer 15 minutes before slicing and serve cold. Serves 10.

★ *Betty Flinn*

FRUIT SHERBET

Cool and refreshing and light.

1	cup water	1	lemon
$^1/_2$	cup sugar	1	egg
1	banana	$^1/_8$	teaspoon salt
1	orange		

Beat egg. Add sugar, water, crushed banana, juice, and pulp of lemon and orange. Mix well. Turn into refrigerator tray and mash well with fork 2-3 times during freezing process. Serves 4.

★*Nancy E. Kehoe*

COFFEE DESSERT

Especially good with rum oranges — see page 179.

$1^1/_2$	cups strong coffee	$^1/_4$	teaspoon salt
$^1/_2$	cup milk	$^1/_2$	teaspoon vanilla
$^1/_3$	cup sugar	1	envelope gelatin
3	eggs		

Dissolve gelatin in milk; add to coffee and sugar. Separate eggs. Put half of salt in egg whites and half in egg yolks. Beat yolks, and add rest of sugar. Add to coffee and cook until thickened. Beat egg whites until stiff. Add coffee mixture to whites slowly, beating all the time. Add vanilla. Rinse a ring mould in cold water. Pour coffee mixture into mould and chill. When serving, decorate with whipped cream. Serves 6-8.

★*Una Redden*

LEMON DESSERT

Light, fresh and festive.

$^3/_4$ **cup sugar**
2 **cups milk**
8 **ounces heavy cream,
   whipped**

**juice and grated rind of
2 lemons**

Blend sugar, milk, lemon rind and juice, and place in freezer. When partly frozen, stir in small carton of cream, whipped. Return to freezer and stir several times. Garnish with cherries or mint leaves. Serves 8-10.

★*Peggy McAlpine*

CHOCOLATE JELLY ROLL

Serve with vanilla ice cream.

4 **eggs**
$^3/_4$ **teaspoon baking powder**
$^3/_4$ **cup sugar**
$^1/_8$ **teaspoon salt**

$^1/_2$ **teaspoon vanilla**
$^1/_2$ **cup cake flour**
$^1/_4$ **cup cocoa**

Beat eggs until very light. Sprinkle baking powder on top and mix well. Gradually add sugar, salt and vanilla and beat until light. Sift together flour and cocoa; add to egg mixture and stir just enough to blend. Pour batter into 15 x 10-inch jelly roll pan and bake at 375°F. for 10 to 12 minutes. While still hot, invert cake onto a sheet of wax paper, thickly spread with icing sugar, and roll up.

★*Thirsty Thinkers Tea Room*

CRAN ACHAN

An old Scottish dessert. It is simple to make and delicious.

whipping cream
coarse oatmeal

castor sugar
rum or brandy or whisky
(rum is best, I think)

Toast some oatmeal lightly before the fire, or in the oven in a thick-bottomed frying-pan over a gentle heat. This gives it a somewhat nutty flavour. Beat a bowlful of cream to a stiff consistency and stir in a handful or two of oatmeal — the cream must predominate. Sweeten to taste and flavour with rum. Throw in a few handfuls of fresh ripe berries — raspberries, strawberries or blackberries and you have a delicious dessert, or, serve the Cran Achan with fresh fruit.

★*Helen Dennis*

LEMON CAKE PIE

Tender, moist and flaky — a simple solution to easy entertaining.

1 **cup sugar**
2 **eggs, separated**
juice and rind of 1 lemon
9-inch unbaked pie shell

3 **tablespoons flour**
3 **tablespoons butter**
1 **cup milk**

Cream sugar, flour and butter. Stir in beaten egg yolks. Add lemon juice and rind and milk, slowly. Beat egg whites until stiff, then fold into mixture. Pour into a 9-inch unbaked pie shell. Bake in 350°F. for about 30 to 40 minutes or until firm and brown.

★*Thirsty Thinkers Tea Room*

RUM ORANGES

Not only a complete dessert in themselves, these oranges are also delicious with other fruit, with ice cream, or with a rum custard sauce.

2 cups sugar	$1/_2$ cup plus 2 tablespoons rum
$3^1/_4$ cups water	6 seedless navel oranges

Put the sugar, water and $1/_2$ cup rum in a pot and bring them to a boil. Reduce the heat, cover the pot, and simmer the syrup for 10 minutes.

Meanwhile, cut off the thick ends of the oranges and discard. Cut the oranges into slices about $1/_4$ inch thick. When the syrup is ready, add the oranges and any juice that may have collected from them. Cover and simmer for 20 minutes.

Remove the pot from the heat, add the remaining 2 tablespoons of rum, re-cover at once, and put aside to cool. Chill in the refrigerator for 2 hours.

Arrange 4 or 5 orange slices on an individual plate. Serves 4.

★*Sally Farrell*

DELUXE PUMPKIN PIE

Have fun — and if you like whipped cream, have lots of napkins on hand!

2	cans pumpkins	2	teaspoons cinnamon
2	teaspoons salt plus a pinch	1	full teaspoon ginger
5	cups evaporated milk	$^1/_2$	teaspoon cloves
6	eggs	$2^1/_4$	cups sugar
3	tablespoons melted butter	2	unbaked pie shells

Beat eggs. Then add sugar, cloves, ginger, cinnamon, salt, and milk. Stir in melted butter. Beat in pumpkin. Pour into 2 unbaked pie shells. Bake for 45 minutes in a 350°F. oven. Top with whipped cream and serve. Serves 12.

★*Ruth Gibson*

EASY SUMMER DESSERT

A great favourite with the kids, and a snap for last-minute company.

1	box yellow cake mix	8	ounces cream cheese
1	pound can of crushed pineapple (drained)	9	ounces Cool Whip coconut and chopped pecans (optional)
3	ounce package instant vanilla pudding		

Bake the mix in a 13 x 2 inch pyrex dish. Cool. Top with pineapple. Mix vanilla pudding and chill for 5 to 10 minutes. Beat the cream cheese until creamy and fluffy. Add the chilled pudding and whip again. Add the Cool Whip. Spread this mixture over the pineapple. Top with coconut and pecans. Serves 6.

★*Betty Flinn*

Preserves

TOMATO RELISH

Very easy to make but full of flavour.

1 large can whole tomatoes	$^1/_2$ cup granulated sugar
1 large onion	2 tablespoons pickling spice
2 stalks celery	salt and pepper, to taste
1 cup vinegar	

Dice onion and celery. Tie pickling spice in a small piece of cotton to prevent it from spilling into mixture. Add other ingredients, and simmer over medium heat until onions and celery are clear. Stir occasionally to prevent sticking.

★ *Regis Dyer*

RIPE UNCOOKED TOMATO RELISH

Almost as good as fresh tomatoes.

20 ripe tomatoes	4 or 5 medium onions
1 green pepper, chopped	2 cups vinegar
$^1/_4$ cup salt	3 cups brown sugar

Combine tomatoes, onions, green pepper and add salt. Hang in a bag overnight to drain. The next morning, put in a bowl and add brown sugar and vinegar. Stir well until sugar dissolves. Put in jars and seal.

★ *Una Redden*

CUCUMBER RELISH

This recipe is very easy to make and one of my great favourites. As well as serving it with fish, I serve it with hamburgers or any type of meat.

12 or 14 large cucumbers, peeled, seeded and diced

4 cups onions, chopped fine
$1/_2$ cup salt

Combine and let stand overnight. Put dish on to heat in the morning. When heated, drain and add to the following mixture, which has been cooked,

1 quart vinegar
5 cups sugar
1 cup flour

1 teaspoon celery seed
1 teaspoon mustard seed
1 teaspoon turmeric

Boil everything together for 10 minutes, then bottle.

★*Mrs. Cavell Stevens*

HOMEMADE CHEESE SPREAD

In these days when we are reading labels and trying to find pure food without additives, here is a recipe for cheese spread made from natural ingredients. It is very inexpensive and very good.

2 cups grated Cheddar cheese
1 tablespoon plain yogurt
$1/_4$ cup apple juice

$1/_2$ teaspoon nutmeg
pinch of cayenne

Mix in blender and refrigerate.

★*Grace McClung*

CANDIED FRUIT PEEL

Candied fruit peel can usually be bought at the Bonny Lea Farm Christmas Bazaar, but it is not difficult to make at home.

2	grapefruit	$^1/_2$	cup corn syrup
1	cup granulated sugar	1	cup water

Cut peel from grapefruit into thin strips (cut away most of the membrane). Cover peel with cold water. Bring to a boil and boil for 10 minutes. Repeat 3 times. In a 3-quart saucepan combine sugar, corn syrup, water. Stir over low heat until sugar dissolves. Add peel — boil gently, uncovered, for 40 minutes or until most of the syrup is absorbed. Drain in strainer or collander. Roll peel in granulated sugar. Let stand 2 days in a single layer on waxed paper.

Orange Fruit Peels
Slice 6 oranges in the same way. Boil peel for 5 minutes. Increase sugar to 2 cups. Decrease syrup to 2 teaspoons. Continue in same manner as for grapefruit.

★ *Grace McClung*

RHUBARB, PINEAPPLE
AND STRAWBERRY JAM

Rhubarb, pineapple, and strawberry flavours go well together.

5 cups rhubarb, cut small	2 packages Strawberry Jello
1 medium can crushed pineapple	5 cups sugar

Put in a kettle. Let stand overnight. In the morning bring to a boil and cook for 20 minutes. Add Strawberry Jello. Stir well, put in jars and seal. Makes about 4 pints.

★ *Una Redden*

RHUBARB JELLY

This rhubarb jelly is delicious with chicken, and tart enough to use if you run out of marmalade for breakfast.

1 pot of rhubarb	$3^1/_2$ cups sugar
$^3/_4$ cup water	1 bottle Certo
$3^1/_2$ cups juice	

Stew rhubarb with water. Let sit overnight. Strain. Heat $3^1/_2$ cups of the juice and add sugar. Bring to a boil, add Certo, bring to a rolling boil for one minute, stirring constantly. Remove from heat. Skim the top with metal spoon, pour into jars, and, when cool, seal.

★ *Mona Campbell*

LEMON CURD

For a really delicious filling for cream puffs, mix equal amounts of lemon curd and whipped cream.

zest of 2 large lemons, removed with vegetable peeler or zester
$^2/_3$ cup sugar

5 large egg yolks
juice of 2 large lemons (about $^1/_2$ cup)
$^1/_2$ cup (1 stick) unsalted butter, melted

In food processor, using steel knife, mince lemon zest with sugar using several on/off turns, then let machine run until zest is of desired fineness. Add yolks and lemon juice and let machine run about 5 seconds to blend. With machine running, pour melted butter through feed tube.

Pour mixture into heavy stainless steel saucepan or stainless or glass top of double boiler. Cook very slowly, mixing constantly with stainless wire whisk or wooden spoon, until thickened — about 10 minutes. Cool, then refrigerate. Yield: $1^1/_3$ cups.

Lemon curd will keep 2 to 3 months, covered and refrigerated.

★ *Valda Ondaatje*

MARGARET'S MINCEMEAT

It is a good idea to have meat and suet minced by a butcher, because it clogs a small mincer. I use minced round steak, cook it in a double boiler, and then cool it.

1	pound suet	1	pound brown sugar
1	pound cooked beef	2	teaspoons salt
1	pound peeled, diced apples	1	teaspoon cloves
		1	teaspoon allspice
1	pound raisins	8	ounces dark rum
1	pound currants		
$^1/_2$	pound citron		

Mince raisins, currants and citron. This can easily be done at home. Place all ingredients in a very large bowl, preparing apples last, as they turn brown quickly.

Pour the rum over the whole mixture. Use both hands to mix, as the batter is very heavy. Cover with waxed paper and store in a covered container. Yield: 6 $^1/_4$ pounds. Merry Christmas!

★ *Elizabeth Pellow*

GRANOLA

Great breakfast cereal with milk and honey or sugar. From Helena.

$^2/_3$ **cup sesame seeds**
$^1/_2$ **cup slivered almonds**
$^1/_2$ **cup shelled sunflower seeds**
$^1/_4$ **cup butter**
$^3/_4$ **cup cashews**

1 **cup unsweetened coconut**
$^1/_3$ **cup light sesame oil**
4 **cups rolled oats**
$^1/_3$ **cup honey**
$^3/_4$ **cup currants or raisins**

Heat oven to 350°F. Dry toast sesame seeds in wok and turn into bowl. Dry toast almonds, add sunflower seeds; brown. Add sesame seeds. Turn into bowl. Melt butter in wok and add cashews. Toast and add coconut. Toast again and add to mixture in bowl. Heat oil in wok and add oats and toast. Add the mixture in bowl and honey. Heat 5 minutes, turning in wok. Turn mixture into a roasting pan and spread evenly. Bake for 10 to 20 minutes or until golden brown. Drain on paper towels. Break into chunks and add either currants or raisins. Store in an airtight jar. You can also add wheat germ, millet or any dried fruit.

★*Eleanor Seyffert*

C-Boat Fever

If you listen very carefully
You can hear the Ripple win
You can hear the sweat and groaning
As they haul the jib sheet in
You can hear the laughter carry
As they catch the western wind
And they ease her past the Mistral,
Past Eclipse, and past the Whim.

Built in Nova Scotia
Nineteen thirty eight
And the stars must have been shining
And they served the rum real late
'Cos they knew what they were doing
On Chester's harbour shore
When they fitted groin to tenon
Ben Heisler knew the score.

Fifty feet of mast head
Five forty feet of sail
Decks of solid pinewood
Built to take the sleet and hail
Sleek just like a kitten
Cutting through the swell
But beating back to windward
Tough as bloody hell.

You can talk of Thomas Lipton
And the Bluenose we will mourn
Sail the sunny tropics
Or rough it round the horn
But when you come home to Race Week
Be prepared to meet your match
'Cos the Ripple's tuned for trouble
You'd better batten down your hatch.

If you listen very carefully
You can hear the Ripple win
You can hear the sweat and groaning
As they haul the jib sheet in
You can hear the laughter carry
As they catch the western wind
And they ease her past the Mistral,
Past Eclipse, and past the Whim;
Past the Gannet, past Sajoda,
Past the Ohop, and back in.

Christopher Ondaatje

Index